Comfort In Captivity

Julia Ulstad

DEDICATION

<u>Comfort in Captivity</u> is dedicated to my 10 year jail ministry buddy, Indira. She is the reason this booklet was compiled and she was a valuable resource for getting others to write their stories. <u>Comfort in Captivity</u> comes from her heart for those in hard places.

ACKNOWLEDGMENTS

Special thanks to my husband, Sam. Without his help this book would not have been written. His computer skills made this project so much easier for me. I would still be trying to figure it all out if it weren't for him. He is a rock!

Thanks also to my "writer" sister Susan Thode, and my "English teacher" daughter Christine Wensley, who were very helpful editors with wonderful suggestions. What a team!

CONTENTS

Ch   Pg

    Introduction ----------------------------- 1

1   Rena's Story ----------------------------- 3
2   Redemption: It's all God's Idea ---------- 8
3   What Is My Part --------------------------- 13
4   The Romans Road ----------------------- 16
5   The Littles ------------------------------- 19
6   Life As I Knew It...But God -------------- 23
7   Deborah -------------------------------- 28
8   Valerie Jane ----------------------------- 31
9   The Holy Spirit - Our Comforter -------- 34
10   Comfort My People --------------------- 38
11   John the Baptist ------------------------- 40
12   Paul and Silas --------------------------- 43
13   The Evangelists -------------------------- 47
14   That Dreamer --------------------------- 50
15   The Den of Lions ------------------------ 53
16   Tim's Story - Comfort in Confinement -- 56
17   True Freedom --------------------------- 59
18   I Doubt That ---------------------------- 65
19   Holly's Story ---------------------------- 69
20   Fear Not --------------------------------- 73
21   Wait...and Pray ------------------------- 78
22   Clair's Story ----------------------------- 84
23   Forgiveness ------------------------------ 87
24   My Journey Through Anxiety and
    Depression ------------------------------ 90
25   Prison to Praise ------------------------- 97
26   Freedom From Any Prison --------------- 101
27   God's War Room ------------------------ 105
28   Paul's War Room ------------------------ 109
29   The Armor of God ----------------------- 112
30   Words of Comfort from Isaiah ----------- 116
31   More Words of Comfort ----------------- 120
    Robins in the Snow ---------------------- 122

INTRODUCTION

The people living in Old Testament Bible times often found themselves desperately needing God's comfort. Many times they were in captivity, under enemy attack, lonely, and hopeless. During these times God sent the prophets to bring words of comfort from Himself. Many people through the ages have found the same comfort from these words of hope and encouragement.

This month-long devotional will look at these words of the prophets as well as words from the New Testament to those of us who are living in some form of captivity due to imprisonment, illness, addiction, loneliness, unhealthy relationships or other causes. Along the way we'll hear personal stories from current and former prisoners and other people in different kinds of captivity who received comfort from Jesus.

The theme of this booklet is from the Prophet Isaiah:

"Comfort, O comfort My people says your God. Speak tenderly to Jerusalem and tell her that her sad days are gone. Her sins are pardoned, and the Lord will give twice as many blessings as he gave her punishment before." Isaiah 40:1-2 The Living Bible*

Webster's dictionary definition for comfort is "to soothe in distress or sorrow, ease the misery or grief of; bring consolation or hope to."

William Barclay, in his commentary on the New Testament book of Acts, says, "The Comforter is the one who fills men with courage and strength."

As we consider God's words of comfort, I pray that God will soothe our sorrow, ease our misery and bring us hope. May He help us all to receive the comfort, strength, and courage that only He can bring.

*All Bible references in this booklet are from the New International Version unless otherwise noted.

1 - RENA'S STORY
by Rena Grace Henderson

I will start my story by saying, I have been where you are: sitting in jail with people staring down at me with hate and anger, judging me and who I was. It was like I wasn't even a person; a real flesh and blood, hurting person.

But I didn't need anyone. I didn't care what people thought. No one cared and I didn't need them or anything else. Or so I told myself.

I could have played the "oh poor me" card. I could have told myself that the justice system was against me, and against everyone in here with me! I believed they were! But I had gotten myself into that mess. I did wrong, I knew I did wrong, and I was being justly punished. I was a broken woman, but unbeknownst to me, something, someone was working in my life. Someone was whispering in that judge's ear when he sent me to a county jail which was far away from the county I lived in. I was to serve a year there.

The third day in jail I was moved into Max. Another inmate had taken food off my plate and I reacted by beating her down! Max - Maximum Security. There I was sitting in that 3 by 8 foot cell with nothing to do for 23 hours of the day; I was nearly driven to the edge. In Max a person has nothing personal with them except a toothbrush. In the morning you are told to roll up your sleeping mat and blanket. It is stored for you in another empty cell so you cannot even sleep the day away. Laying on that cold metal bed frame during the boring daylight hours of nothingness seemed endless. Throughout the day a guard would come along and bang on my cell door to wake me up should I fall asleep.

Inmates in Max would get out of their small cells for an hour a day. For that hour I could sit alone, read a book, or take a shower. Within a week an idea hit me; I asked the guard if I could read for my hour. I had a Bible in my property, which was my personal belongings, and was allowed to have it for the hour. This Bible had been given to me when I was in a foster home at the age of 14. It had not been read or even looked at. For some reason, as I headed for court on the day I was sentenced, I picked up the Bible and slipped it into my purse. I now know the reason I took it with me!

As I spent my hour reading God's Word, a plan materialized in my mind. When the hour was up and I had to put my Bible away, I carefully hid it in my bedroll in the empty cell where my property was stored. After my dinner was brought I waited the hour until my bedroll was given to me in exchange for my empty plate. Bible reading began in earnest that night.

Every night I would read, listening for the jangle of the keys that let me know a guard was coming. I slid the Bible under me and pretended to be asleep until the guard moved on. Every night was the same except that I started taking notes with a pencil stub and paper I had recovered from my stuff. Eventually I began to really READ the Bible. Every morning I would roll up my Bible with my bedroll and sleep as much as I could on the hard metal bed frame while I waited for nighttime.

It was at night, alone and lost, that God's Word started to penetrate my soul. And I heard Him! Faintly at first; soft, touches, gentle caresses, love floating across my being, and into my mind. That is what happened to me: I found my lost love in that cell in Max. I connected with my Father, Brother, Lord, Lover, and Savior. God's Spirit flowed out of my Bible, each word opening me up so He could get in.

Later, after getting out of Max, I met the woman who would be the hand of God for me. That woman would show me how to be a friend, how a lady acts, and what God's light could be in my life. God used her to help me be a better "Me". She became my friend, my sister, my mother, and a rock in my life. After ten years she is still my friend even though we live miles apart.

When I got out of Max I started going to the Sunday Services, where I met my new friend. I signed up to receive visits with her and attended any Bible studies that I could. I started loving those women around me who needed Jesus in their lives. I was allowed to participate in water baptism in a jail bathtub with love in my heart and the Jail Administrator in attendance!

Having Jesus in my life did not make jail easy, but I was a brand new person and had a much better focus, and a mission! I could be "Jesus in jail" to those around me.

I discovered I had an enemy, not of flesh and blood, but spiritual. Satan wasn't happy about his loss of a soul in the kingdom of darkness, and began to whisper lies in my ear. The battle began right after my baptism. This enemy used a guard: "Baptized tonight? Jail for Jesus. Wasted on you! You'll be back here again, and then it will be Jesus in jail again. I've seen it all the time."

Lights off and Satan came himself to whisper in my ear, "She's right. Do you think a little water changed anything? Think you are worth love?"

One thought, one Bible passage came to me: "Get thee behind me, Satan!" He left that night, but returned to visit me daily. It was a daily battle, but Jesus fought for me and helped me in the battle.

When I left the county jail one of the guards looked at me and said, "I'll see you again and you can find Jesus again!" I looked at her and smiled because I knew: I was "Jesus in jail" and I could be "Jesus in the world."

I owe Him everything. I was a lost sinner, worthy of nothing. Jesus had died for me, and He came for me, gave me His love and a second chance. He will also enable me to be like

Him, and like my new mom, to be "Jesus" in the world.

It can be in a cold, hard cell that the Lord God will come to heal your soul and fill you with love; and begin to mold you into who He wants you to be. He's still with me and I know will never leave me!   -Rena-

"The Spirit of the Sovereign Lord is on me, because the Lord has anointed me to preach good news to the poor. He has sent me to bind up the brokenhearted, to proclaim freedom for the captives and release from darkness for the prisoners ... to comfort all who mourn, and provide for those who grieve ... to bestow on them a crown of beauty instead of ashes, the oil of gladness instead of mourning, and a garment of praise instead of a spirit of despair. They will be called oaks of righteousness, a planting of the Lord for the display of his splendor." Isaiah 61:1-3

As Isaiah's message about Jesus says, Rena found that the Spirit of the Lord brought good news to her. He healed her broken heart, released her captive heart, comforted her and brought her joy. He came to do the same for each of us.

In the next few chapters we'll see how Jesus rescues and calls each one of us.

2 - REDEMPTION: IT'S ALL GOD'S IDEA

How does THAT work? Rena found something that she was not looking for, and did not ask for.

"I revealed myself to those who did not ask for me; I was found by those who did not seek me." Isaiah 65:1

How DOES that work? I found something I was not looking for and did not ask for? That is what God says!

We are born in sin. That is, we are born with a sinful nature. Our tendency is to sin, which is rebellion against God. We are naturally self-centered, self-absorbed, self-willed, selfish: everything about us revolves around "self". It is called "original sin". The effect of sin is that it separates us from God, who is good and completely perfect, without sin. We are helplessly controlled by our nature, selfishly inclined to do what seems best for ourselves rather than what we know to be right and good. In fact, Ephesians 2:1 tells us, "As for you, you were dead in your transgressions and sins." That's pretty far gone. DEAD. Spiritually dead.

The dead can do nothing to revive themselves. That is why Jesus said, "You must be born again." John 3:7   Jesus' plan for us to come alive spiritually is not for us to fix ourselves up. His plan is for us to be reborn with a new nature.

We may have heard a very convincing explanation of the

Gospel: God's plan to rescue us from our sinful selves, through faith in what Jesus has done for us. We may have read the Gospel directly from the Bible or another book. We may have believed in Jesus from a young age. There are many ways God reaches His Hand of love toward us.

In our minds we may think **we decided** to trust in God and follow Him, accepting that Jesus died in our place to pay the price of sin. Not so: the Bible says that it is God who decides. It is God who chooses us. John 15:16 says, "You did not choose me, but I chose you..."

What a relief! We don't have to do anything to be chosen. The Bible tells us God chose us before He created the world. "For He chose us in him before the creation of the world to be holy and blameless in his sight." Ephesians 1:4   All we do is respond to God when the Holy Spirit stirs our hearts. Even our ability to respond to God comes from Him! Romans 12:3 says that He gives us "a measure of faith", the faith we need to say "yes" to Him.

In the 3rd chapter of John, Jesus speaks of the Spirit of God as the wind. "The wind blows wherever it pleases. You hear the sound, but you cannot tell where it comes from or where it is going. So it is with everyone born of the Spirit." John 3:8   The Spirit draws us to God and we respond to Him.

A baby cannot decide to be born. In the same way a person

cannot decide to be born again, which is what must happen for us to have eternal life with God. The good news is that if you are reading this the Holy Spirit is very near, and God is calling to you as He once called to me at the age of ten. He gave His grace to me so that I could respond to His call and receive salvation through Jesus Christ. Don't worry that God may not choose you. If He is stirring your heart, He is calling and His desire is for you.

When I was a teen-ager I heard about a poem called, "The Hound of Heaven." It is a very long classic poem written by Francis Thompson in 1893. The poem shows God relentlessly seeking a person (who represents all of us), but that person is running away from God. The metaphor of God as a hound on the hunt and the hunted, each one of us, trying to outrun Him, is very intriguing. I think it is pretty accurate.

Mary Oliver, who wrote an interpretation of the poem, says it is "a truly beautiful poem about how we try to find happiness in all the wrong places when God is the source of our happiness." If you enjoy poetry and have access to the internet, you can find "The Hound of Heaven". It is not an easy read, but Mary can help with understanding it if you want to give it a try. I will leave you with the first verse:

The Hound of Heaven

I fled Him, down the nights and down the days;
I fled Him, down the arches of the years:
I fled Him down the labyrinthine ways
Of my own mind; and in the midst of tears
I hid from Him, and under running laughter,
Up vistaed hopes I sped;
And shot, precipitated,
Adown Titanic glooms of chasmed fears,
From those strong Feet that followed after.*
But with unhurrying chase,
And unperturbed pace,
Deliberate speed, majestic instancy,
They beat -- and a Voice beat
More instant than the Feet--
"All things betray thee, who betrayest Me."

labyrinthine - intricate or involved, twisting
vistaed - as seen in a distant view
precipitated - falling, flowing, or rushing with steep descent
chasmed - as of a deep cleft or gorge

*[The "strong Feet followed after" the man slowly and deliberately, and unperturbed.]

This is our amazing, determined, full-of-love-for-us God. He pursues and pursues and pursues. "If a man has a hundred sheep and one of them gets lost, what will he do? Won't he

leave the ninety-nine others in the wilderness and go and search for the one that is lost until he finds it? And when he has found it, he will joyfully carry it home on his shoulders."
Luke 15:4-5 New Living Translation

3 - WHAT IS MY PART

Why did God choose any of us? I don't know, but I can't get over the fact that He chose me! James I. Packer

We've determined through God's Word that He chose us. He also CALLS those He has chosen. "I am the Lord, the God of Israel, who calls you by name." Isaiah 45:3 There are many ways God calls us; there are no barriers large enough or strong enough to keep God from calling those He has chosen. He does whatever He has to do. I've been amazed at what some people have gone through before yielding to God's call. In the following chapters we will explore some of those personal journeys.

Have you heard the call of God to you? Do you hear it now? Your part is to say "yes". God has already given you the faith to do that. "...think of yourself with sober judgment in accordance with the measure of faith God has given you." Romans 12:3

Genesis 1:2 tells us that "the earth was formless and empty, darkness was over the surface of the deep, and the Spirit of God was hovering over the waters." God had already created the heavens and the earth, but that was just the start of His awesome creative power. The creation was not yet what it would become, "and the Spirit of God was hovering over the waters."

The imagery of Genesis 1:2 gives us a picture of what we are like before receiving the gift of salvation from God. He has created humankind, but we are truly "formless and empty" until He creates in us a new heart (heart meaning the spiritual part of us). "I will give them an undivided heart and put a new spirit in them: I will remove from them their heart of stone and give them a heart of flesh. Then they will follow my decrees and be careful to follow my laws. They will be my people and I will be their God." Ezekiel 11:19-20, and "I will give them a heart to know me, that I am the Lord..." Jeremiah 24:7

God is so faithful to hover over those He is calling. He coaxes and urges us; He seeks us and woos us. He loves us and longs for us to respond to Him. Jesus says that God "draws" us. "No one can come to me unless the Father who sent me draws Him." John 6:44   "The Lord your God is with you, he is mighty to save. He will take great delight in you, he will quiet you with his love, he will rejoice over you with singing." Zephaniah 3:17   Wow! He rejoices over you and over me with singing. He rejoices over us!

Our part? Say yes to God's call! The sobering aspect of this process every believer participates in is that we CAN say no! Say no to God? A friend of mine says, "The only thing we can do on our own [without His help] is to say 'no' to God." Instead of yielding to God and the Kingdom of God, we can yield to Satan and the kingdom of darkness. That is a terrifying thought!

William Barclay says this about what Jesus said in John 6:65; "...no one can come to me unless the Father has enabled him."

"No man can accept Jesus unless he is moved by the Spirit of God to do so, but to the end of the day a man can resist that Spirit, and such a man is not shut out by God; he is shut out by himself" (W. Barclay).

This is the consequence of saying no to God's call. We shut God out! May God help us to always say yes to Him.

How and why does a person say "yes" to God? Paul's letter to the Church in Rome gives a clear explanation of why we need God and how we can say "yes" to God's plan for us.

The next devotional "The Romans Road" is a clear summary of the Gospel of Jesus Christ and how anyone can respond to it.

4 - THE ROMANS ROAD

Quite a long time ago someone showed me The Romans Road, so-named because it is found in the book of Romans. Maybe you have walked that road in the past. It is a unique way to look at the Gospel message of Jesus Christ, from Paul's letter to the Roman Christians. Walk along with me.

As it is written: "There is no one righteous, not even one." Roman's 3:10   The reason that statement is true is explained in Romans 3:23, "for all have sinned and fall short of the glory of God." Since we all are born with a sin nature we all are sinners and none are righteous (holy). Romans 5:12 adds more: "Therefore, just as sin entered the world through one man [Adam] and death through sin, and in this way death came to all men because all have sinned." The death spoken of here is both physical death and spiritual death. Remember, Paul said in Ephesians 2:1 "...you were dead in your transgressions and sins..." To make our status in life without God very clear, Paul says in Romans 6:23,"For the wages of sin is death, but the gift of God is eternal life in Jesus Christ our Lord." Hallelujah! Praise be to God for His wonderful gift to us!

Back to the Romans Road: Paul continues with the Gospel (good news) in Romans 5:8 "But God demonstrated His own love for us in this: while we were yet sinners, Christ died for us." We just read that the wages (penalty) of sin is death, but Jesus died in our place: all of us who say "yes" to God.

There is more good news in <u>Romans 10:13</u>, "...for everyone who calls on the name of the Lord [Jesus] will be saved." God is not partial; He is willing for everyone to be saved and live with Him forever. In fact, it's His desire that everyone would say yes to the salvation He offers.

To sum it all up Paul tells us in <u>Romans 10:9-10</u>, "If you confess with your mouth, 'Jesus is Lord,' and believe in your heart that God raised Him from the dead, you will be saved. For it is with your heart that you believe and are justified, and it is with your mouth that you confess and are saved. As the Scripture says, 'Everyone who trusts in Him will never be put to shame.'" Isaiah 28:16

Centuries before Jesus was born the prophet Isaiah foretold many specific things about Jesus: details about His mother and His ancestry, where He would live, how He would die, even details about His tomb. Isaiah was right about everything he predicted. We can trust that Isaiah was also right about this: putting our trust in Jesus is a sure thing! If we confess and believe, we are saved!

Dear God I know I am a sinner and that there is nothing I can do to save myself. I thank you that Jesus Christ died to pay the price for me. I accept your gift of forgiveness and eternal life in Heaven. I ask you to forgive my sins and help me to live for you.

If you prayed these words now or a prayer like it long ago, you are born again. You have received by faith the gift of God. The Spirit of God lives in you to help you live for Him.

Celebrating your new birth, there is a party going on in Heaven! "There is more rejoicing in Heaven over one sinner who repents than over ninety-nine righteous persons who do not need to repent." Luke 15:7

5 - THE LITTLES

A few months ago we visited my niece and nephew in Texas. As we were ready to go sightseeing one day, my nephew's wife said, "I'll go get the littles," referring to my great-niece and three great-nephews who were off playing somewhere. "The littles." I smiled. We have a Heavenly Father who probably thinks of us as "the littles".

Our God is quite tenderhearted toward children. In the historical books of the Bible (Genesis through Esther) when God refers to His people, His words often include, "all their little ones" or "and your little ones." He makes special mention of the children.

In the New Testament we find that Jesus is especially fond of children. In Mark 10:14 He says, "Let the little children come to me, and do not hinder them." The Greek words used here actually mean, "darling little children." In Galatians 4:19, Paul refers to Jesus' followers as, "my dear children." The Apostle John addresses his hearers as "my little children" (I John 2:1) and "little children" through-out his letter. John has God's heart of affection towards his audience and towards us as well.

It gives me comfort to know that God thinks of me as His "darling little child" even though I don't often feel so darling.

We ARE the littles, and He is BIG! As the song, "Jesus Loves Me," says, "I am weak, but He is strong." Big and Strong! Normally the littles look at their parents and others in their lives with complete trust. Unless that trust has been broken they continue to trust them throughout their lives. And when trust has been broken these little ones still long to trust.

God's trustworthiness can never be broken. He is utterly trustworthy. Good people who love us will fail us. But God is not capable of failing us. "God IS love." 1 John 4:8   As littles we can always know that "when I am afraid, I will trust in You." Psalm 5:3   He instructs us in Proverbs 29:25, "The fear of man brings a snare, but whoever leans on, trusts in, and puts confidence in the Lord is safe." The Amplified Bible

Children need adults, even when they think they don't! That is, they need adults who are grown ups; people who love them and do what is right. They need adults who know how to navigate through life, making good decisions. How much more do we all need God! God knows the past and the future; He knows what will benefit us and what will harm us. God, who knows the future and loves us perfectly, will lead and guide us if we surrender our lives to Him and follow Him along life's sometimes difficult path, in the pleasant times and in the heartaches. Seeing myself as a "little" is comforting. This is how our relationship with God is supposed to be. He is bigger, smarter, stronger... all-powerful; the Bible says that nothing is too difficult for Him (Jeremiah 32:17).   Not only that, Jesus says in Matthew 11:25, "...I praise you, Father, Lord of heaven and earth, because You have hidden these things from the wise and learned, and have revealed them to little children...." God tells the littles his secrets!

In Psalm 131:1 David expressed what his position with God looked like: "My heart is not proud, O Lord, my eyes are not haughty; I do not concern myself with great matters or things too wonderful for me. But I have stilled and quieted my soul like a weaned child with its mother, like a weaned child is my soul within me." (NIV notes: "a child of 4 or 5 who walks trustingly beside its mother.") King David considered himself as a little child before God. David was a "little". He depended on God for everything. God wants to be our loving & kind Father. What a place of security and comfort for us.

"Jesus loves me this I know.
For the Bible tells me so.
Little ones to Him belong
They are weak but He is strong."

"He tends his flock like a shepherd; he gathers the lambs in his arms and carries them close to his heart; he gently leads those that have young." Isaiah 40:11 NIV

"Tell me what to do, O Lord, and make it plain because I am surrounded by waiting enemies. Don't let them get me, Lord! Don't let me fall into their hands! The Living Bible

"You have made known to me the path of life, you will fill me with joy in your presence, with eternal pleasures at your right hand." Psalm 16:11 NIV

How do these words of comfort from God fit with the harsh reality of life? Following are some stories from the lives of real people who are, or have been in captivity. Let's read how those in prison and those facing great difficulties have found God to be present with them in the midst of trying and sometimes heartbreaking circumstances. The next chapter is Gerry's story.

6 - LIFE AS I KNEW IT...BUT GOD
by Gerry McIvor

I grew up in a dysfunctional family setting and lifestyle. Consequently my life was filled with a lot of disappointment and a whole lot of suffering because of my poor decisions. I had been abused by my mother & father from the age of three to thirteen years so my life was set on a terrible path of pain which was very destructive, not only to me but to others. Due to my way of thinking and the way I was living I brought this same hurt and pain to other people who had crossed my path. I arrived at a devastating frame of mind and began to think such things as, "Is this all that life has to offer me?"

I believed there was a God but had no knowledge of how to know this God, or how to experience a personal relationship with Jesus Christ. During my continuing downward spiral, at the darkest time of my life, I thought that the only way out of all the hurt and pain was to end my life. I came to this conclusion because I had my focus on the wrong things. I was following in my parents' footsteps which was to please themselves and to seek only their own pleasure. Like them I was listening to the wrong voices.

I now know what the Bible teaches. Jesus said in John 10:10 and 27, "The thief comes only to steal and kill and destroy; I have come that they might have life, and have it to the full ... My sheep listen to **my voice**." I Peter 5:8 says, "Be self-controlled and alert. Your enemy the devil prowls around like a roaring lion looking for someone to devour." My life had come very close to being devoured.

One night, after a long day of work, my thoughts hit a new low. I was convinced there was no way my life would improve. I was feeling overwhelmed, and decided to quit living. Ending up with a loaded gun pointed at my head, my intention was to end it all. Helplessly I cried out to a God I had believed was real but did not know. This turned out to be the most important thing I had ever done. As I was crying out to God I pulled the trigger.

But something astronomical happened! And I am here to tell about it! As I pulled the trigger of that gun I heard the sound of the hammer slapping against the pin. I was so surprised! I was still here! So I pulled the hammer back a second time and opened my front door. I pointed the gun into the sky and pulled the trigger. It went off! At that moment I knew there was a loving God who heard my cry for help, and he had answered me. I was not a child of God yet, but I wanted to be one. God showed up, and from that day forth I knew God was alive and well and that he loved me.

He saved me from physical death as well as the spiritual death I had pursued for so long. Why? God heard my cry for help! Revelation 3:20 says, "Here I am. I stand at the door and knock. If anyone hears my voice and opens the door, I will come in and eat with him and he with me."

"For the Son of Man came to seek and to save what was lost." Luke 19:10   "The righteous cry out, and the Lord hears them; he delivers them from all their troubles." Psalm 34:17

I was at the point where I could do nothing but cry out and humble myself to an all-knowing God who heard my cries of desperation. He saved me. He is faithful - a God who loves us, and comes to our rescue in our moment of need. His timing is right and always perfect. He is alive and well this very day! He is a God of hope who we can trust and rely on in every circumstance. I am here to say that this God wants a personal relationship with you! He desires it.

From the point of my near death encounter I became a believer in God, the One who is worthy of our praise and worship. He is a caring God who came to save us not to destroy us. "For God did not send his Son into the world to condemn the world, but to save the world through him." John 3:17

"Without faith it is impossible to please God, because anyone who comes to Him must believe that he exists and that He rewards those who diligently seek him." Hebrews 11:6   I trust and believe in his word that brings life and encouragement to my days. Since giving my life to Him my days now have purpose. It is God who plans my days. It is God who guides and directs my footsteps. "'For I know the plans I have for you,' declares the Lord, 'plans to give you a hope and a future.'" Jeremiah 29:11, "In his heart a man

plans his course, but the Lord determines his steps."
Proverbs 16:9

We are all living in this world, but we don't have to be like the world. "Do not conform any longer to the pattern of this world, but be transformed by the renewing of your mind. Then you will be able to test and approve what God's will is -- his good , pleasing, and perfect will." Romans 1:2

We can stay encouraged when we stop to listen to the STORY of others. God's Story. We can become the voice of God to everyone who needs Him. Take a minute in this fast paced life, and see the movement of God. Hear about the amazing things He is doing, restoring the lives of lost (unsaved) people. He is the God we call Jesus Christ. Come to know Him more intimately. He wants to take on what we cannot handle on our own. John 14:16-27 "I can do everything through him who strengthens me." Philippians 4:13

God wants us to quit listening to the wrong voices and quit putting our eyes on wrong things, these things that God calls sin: the things that will eventually destroy us. We have options; we can serve God who cares about us and will give us all we need to do His will. And we can become light for others. He will answer our questions. He did mine!

God gave me a second chance at life. Now I want to live a life pleasing to Him, the One who brought hope and purpose into my life. The reason for this devotional is that there are still people who live in circumstances of confinement or of struggles without knowing the Good News. Many may be in a place they do not want to be. These written pages contain good news of love and hope for you. All of us who have written our stories know that it is only by God's grace that we are saved and restored. It is never by anything that we have done (even good things), but by the unconditional and unfathomable love of God, through the sacrifice of Jesus Christ.

Praise be to Jesus Christ who saved me, and continues to save all who will turn to Him. You can have this same life. It is for all who want it, and it is free!

Gerry gives his time each week visiting men in his local Michigan county jail.

7 - DEBORAH

"Village life in Israel ceased, ceased until I, Deborah, arose, arose a mother in Israel." Judges 5:7

One of my favorite Old Testament stories in the Bible is the story of Deborah, found in the book of Judges, chapters 4 & 5.

The book of Judges gives the historical accounts of the judges who led God's people after the death of Joshua who had become the leader of the Israelites after Moses died. This period of history lasted until the establishment of the monarchy, starting with King Saul.

Deborah was one of the judges appointed by God. He chose Deborah, a woman, because He is God and she was who He wanted to lead His people. This was a time in history when women were usually powerless and marginalized. God's choice of Deborah makes me think of the Scripture verse in Galatians 3:26-28 "You are all sons of God through faith in Christ Jesus, for all of you who were baptized into Christ have clothed yourselves with Christ. There is neither Jew nor Greek, slave nor free, male nor female, for you are all one in Christ Jesus." God doesn't value us based on our race, social status or gender. He values us simply because we are His "littles." What a comforting verse that is!

Deborah was created by God with unique gifts and talents, as we all are. This critical time in history was the time God wanted to use her to accomplish His will. I hope you read the short story of Deborah. Chapter 4 of Judges gives the historical account, and chapter 5 contains "The Song of Deborah", which tells the story in a song. There were two women who were heroes on the day of battle. Besides Deborah there was Jael, the woman who killed Sisera, the commander of the army opposing the Israelites!

We have already seen from the Bible that God is the One who chooses those who will belong to Him. "I revealed myself to those who did not ask for me; I was found by those who did not seek me." Isaiah 65   Once we surrender our lives to God there are other choices He makes. He has a plan for each person who accepts Him. Jeremiah 29:11 tells us that God says, "'For I know the plans I have for you,' declares the Lord, 'plans to prosper you and not to harm you, plans to give you hope and a future.'" God wants good for each of us. He wants to use us in His Kingdom. Our part is to follow Him as He shows us His will for us. God has gifted each of us and will equip us to follow Him.

Galatians 3:28 (see page 2<del>9</del>8) emphasizes that God places no limitations on us because of social status, race or gender. We are all gifted by God for a purpose and He will show us that purpose.

One of my favorite Scriptures is from the prophet Micah. "He has showed you O man, what is good. And what does the Lord require of you? To act justly and to love mercy and to walk humbly with your God." Micah 6:8

Sometimes following those instructions is not easy, but the good news is that God never asks us to do anything that He won't help us do. "For it is God who works in you to will and to act according to His good purpose." Philippians 2:13 and, "...being confident of this, that he who began a good work in you will carry it on to completion until the day of Christ Jesus." Philippians 1:6

Deborah's story shows us that God chooses those who society would push aside, that He accomplishes good in this world through very unlikely people. And the outcome is not up to us. We follow God's call and He works in us to complete His good works inside of us, and then through us as we walk humbly with Him.

8 - VALERIE JANE

Meet Valerie Jane (not her real name).

She lives in prison. Valerie Jane and I write letters to each other. She is a mother and has a wonderful husband who visits her regularly along with her children. Although Valerie is not able to be a mother to her own family the way she would like to be, God has given her many women to "mother" where she is. I think of her as a "Mother in Israel".

Valerie goes out of her way to comfort and encourage the women around her, especially the new women coming into her area. In the prison there are some wonderful Christian resources and programs available, so she helps introduce the new women to them.

Valerie wrote to me recently about her experience speaking to a group of women. Her topic was about how God uses Christians to help others. The role-model of her talk was a woman from the New Testament named Dorcus. Valerie wrote that, "Dorcus was a giving, caring kind of woman. She had a reputation for being compassionate, resourceful and generous." V.J. pointed out that, "Dorcus, like many who serve others, put the others before herself."

According to the Bible account, Dorcus became ill, and died. However, the story has a happy ending;   you will want to read it! (Acts 9:36-41) "We can learn from this story that as we help others we must take care of ourselves also," says V.J. "We do this by letting God refresh us, and also allow others to help us." We need our time alone with God just as Jesus did. The Bible says Jesus often went off by Himself to pray to his Father. If Jesus needed communication and strengthening from God, how much more do we need it!

"They that wait upon the Lord shall renew their strength. They shall mount up with wings like eagles; they shall run and not be weary; they shall walk and not faint." Isaiah 40:31 The Living Bible   And how about this promise from God: "No mere man has ever seen, heard or imagined what wonderful things God has for those who love the Lord. But we know about these things because God has sent his Spirit to tell us, and his Spirit searches out and tells us all of God's deepest secrets." I Corinthians 2:9-10 The Living Bible   And John tells us this: "They will all be taught by God. Everyone who listens to the Father and learns from him comes to me." John 6:45 The Living Bible

Isaiah says in chapter 50, verse 4, "The Lord has given me words of wisdom so that I may know what I should say to all these weary ones." The Living Bible   When we are weary it is so comforting to know that God is on our side, that His thoughts are on us.

I love these encouraging words that V.J. left with her group of women: "God never forgets a labor of love. My sister,

God has not forgotten your ministry and we all have one: from sharing the Word of God, to feeding someone who is hungry, and being there when someone is in need. You may help someone who then rises up, walks away, and forgets to thank you for your sacrifice. Not God! He never forgets, and just when you need Him most He will show up. You know the times when you thought, 'Who is going to see about me?' And then you are asked if you are okay, 'Do you need anything, can I help you?'"   Valerie Jane

I hope you have a Valerie Jane in your life, or maybe you are one! God Bless all the mothers in captivity!

Think about the following verses and ask God how you can be like a trusted parent to those around you. How can God's faithfulness come to others through you? Ask Him to lift and carry you in His love and mercy.

"The faithful love of the Lord never ends! His mercies never cease. Great is his faithfulness; his mercies begin again each morning." Lamentations 3:22-23 New Living Translation.

"In all their suffering he also suffered. He personally rescued them. In his love and mercy he redeemed them. He lifted them up and carried them through all the years." Isaiah 54.9 New Living Translation

9 - THE HOLY SPIRIT - OUR COMFORTER

Watchman Nee was a true hero of the faith who was imprisoned in Communist China in 1952, and died there in 1972. Nee knew what it was to suffer under harsh prison conditions. I recommend to you any of his writings. In his devotional book, A Table in the Wilderness, he tells a story to illustrate the gift of the Holy Spirit for Christians:

"Suppose I went into a bookshop, selected a two-volume book, and having put down the price, walked out of the shop, carelessly leaving one volume on the counter. When I discovered the oversight, what should I do? I should go straight back to recover the forgotten volume, but I ought not to dream of paying anything for it. I should simply remind the shopkeeper that both volumes were duly paid for, thank him again for the second one, and without further ado march happily out of the shop with my possession under my arm. Would you not do the same under the same circumstances?"

"But you are under the same circumstances. If you have fulfilled the conditions you are entitled to two gifts, not just one. You have already taken the remission of your sins. Why not just come, and if you have never done so, thank him for the gift of the Holy Ghost [Holy Spirit] now?

'Repent ye, and be baptized every one of you in the name of Jesus Christ unto the remission of your sins: and you shall receive the gift of the Holy Ghost.' Acts 2:28"

In the Bible, the book of Acts is the record of the birth of the Christian Church and of the years that follow. It is a history book written 60 to 70 years after the birth of Christ. The 2nd chapter of Acts tells of the coming of The Holy Spirit. Before Jesus was taken back to Heaven He had instructed his followers to wait in Jerusalem to be "baptized with the Holy Spirit." Acts 1:1-14   You will want to read the first two chapters of Acts, maybe the whole book of Acts!

Throughout the story in Acts we see that once people come to believe in Jesus they also receive the gift of the Holy Spirit. We also see that it happened in different ways for different people. in Acts 10 and 11 we see people who hear Peter speaking to different groups about Jesus, the people believing in Jesus, receiving His salvation and receiving the gift of the Holy Spirit.

In another story we see Paul encounter a group of people who had heard of Jesus through the preaching of John the Baptist. They said to Paul, "We have not even heard that there is a Holy Spirit." Acts 19:1-2   But when Paul tells them the whole story, they believe and are filled with the Holy Spirit. The Book of Acts is an entire book filled with the work of the Holy Spirit in and through the people who follow Jesus. Jesus was an seemingly insignificant Jewish man who was eventually executed by the Roman government. Yet in Acts we see that His story becomes known throughout the world through the power of the Holy Spirit.

The preaching of the Gospel or good news, was and is now a two-volume book, as in Watchman Nee's illustration. Jesus isn't able to be physically present with all of His followers, but He has given us a wonderful gift; the Spirit of God who is present with each of, living in us who are believers in Him.

After the Resurrection of Jesus from the grave he told his disciples this, "And I will ask the Father, and He will give you another Comforter (Counselor, Strengthener, Advocate, Helper and Standby) that He may remain with you forever." John 14:16 Amplified Version   He is all of those names because He is so much bigger that just one of them! My favorite is the Comforter.

A classic hymn, *The Comforter Has Come*, captures the essence of our Comforter:

> O spread the tidings round wherever man is found,
> Wherever human hearts and human woes abound;
> Let every Christian tongue proclaim the joyful sound:
> The Comforter has come!

The long, long night is past, the morning breaks at last,
And hushed the dreadful sound and fury of the blast,
As over golden hills the day advances fast
The Comforter has come!

Lo, the great King of kings, with healing in His wings,
To every captive soul a full deliverance brings;
And through the vacant cells the song of triumph rings:
The Comforter has come!

O boundless love divine! How Shall this tongue of mine
To wondering mortals tell the matchless grace divine
That I, a child of hell, should in His image shine?
The Comforter has come!

Chorus

The Comforter has come, the Comforter has come!
The Holy Ghost from Heaven, the Father promise given;
O spread the tidings round wherever man is found
The Comforter has come!

.............Francis Bottome

The Comforter has come! He came during the time of Acts. And He is here today. He comforts us; He brings life to us; and He is God's very presence with us. No matter what we've done or the difficulty of our circumstances if we have received Jesus Christ as our Savior, the Holy Spirit lives in us to comfort us, to help us and to show us God's will!

10 - COMFORT MY PEOPLE

It is no surprise that the prophet who conveyed God's desire to bring comfort to His people gives us a detailed description of the Spirit of God, the Holy Spirit, who lives in us. As there are many names for the Holy Spirit (Comforter, Counselor, Advocate, Helper...), there are attributes (special powers) that Isaiah names to show how awesome our Lord is. Everything we need to comfort and fulfill us is available to us through the Holy Spirit in us.

Isaiah 11:2 says, "The Spirit of the Lord will rest on him (Jesus) - the Spirit of wisdom and of understanding, the Spirit of counsel and of power, the Spirit of knowledge and of the fear of the Lord." This is the same Spirit who makes a home in you and in me when we accept Jesus as our Savior!

Many books have been written about The Holy Spirit; there is so much to say about Him! I just want to try to briefly explain what is written in this one verse from Isaiah so we can understand a little bit of what we have when The Holy Spirit lives in us.

1 and 2. The Spirit of wisdom and the Spirit of understanding work together to give believers the ability to discern (recognize) the good or evil nature of things, and know the differences in things and situations we encounter.

3.   The Spirit of <u>counsel</u> is the gift of forming right conclusions.

4.   The Spirit of <u>might</u> is the ability to carry out the right conclusions with energy.

5.   The Spirit of the <u>knowledge of God</u> is knowing God, founded on a relationship of love of God, and an awareness of God.

6.   The Spirit of the <u>fear of the Lord</u> is awe and reverence (honor and respect) of God that inspires obedience. Even Jesus obeyed God, "The One who sent me is with me; he has not left me alone, for I always do what pleases him." John 8:29

This little trip into the area of theology (the study of God), is meant to show us what tremendous gifts we receive through The Holy Spirit. We are never really alone for the Comforter is ours and lives in us. Isaiah said, "When you go through deep waters and great trouble, I will be with you. When you go through rivers of difficulty, you will not drown! When you walk through the fires of oppression, you will not be burned up -- the flames will not consume you. --Don't be afraid, for I am with you." Isaiah 43:1-2 (check out 5-7 also) The Living Bible

11 - JOHN THE BAPTIST

Soon after the Angel Gabriel visited Mary with the news that she would give birth to the Son of God, Mary journeyed to visit her relative, Elizabeth. At the time, Elizabeth was six months pregnant with her son, John (Luke 1:5-38). We are not told the reason for the visit, but she may have wanted to seek counsel and encouragement from Elizabeth and her husband, Zechariah the priest. One of the most important things we can learn about Mary is her response to the news the angel brought to her. "'I am the Lord's servant,' Mary answered. 'May it be to me as you have said.'" Luke 1:38

When Mary arrived at Elizabeth's home, and the two women greeted each other, the Bible says this: "When Elizabeth heard Mary's greeting, the baby [John] leaped in her womb and Elizabeth was filled with the Holy Spirit. In a loud voice she exclaimed: 'Blessed are you among women, and blessed is the child you will bear!'" Luke 1:41-42   What follows is Mary's Song. (Luke 1:46-55)   In this expression of worship, Mary thanks God for His mighty acts and for how He has lifted up a mere teen-age girl to be used to fulfill His promise to His people. Mary returned to Nazareth about three months later, and soon after she left, John was born to Elizabeth and Zechariah.

After John grew up and left home, his life was not easy. He traveled, preaching in the Desert of Judea, calling people to repent from their sins. He baptized those who repented, and he prophesied about the coming of Jesus. One day when John was baptizing people in the Jordan River, Jesus came to him and asked to be baptized (Mt 3:1-17). Shortly after John baptized Him, Jesus public ministry began.

John continued his ministry of calling people to repentance and baptizing them. Because John preached the truth about sin and the hypocrisy of the religious leaders, some of those leaders became angry and persuaded the Roman authorities to arrest and imprison him.

"After John was put in prison, Jesus went into Galilee, proclaiming the good news of God. 'The time has come,' he said, 'the kingdom of God is near. Repent and believe the good news!'" Mark 1:14-15   Jesus spoke to the people about the ministry of John (John 1:6-9), and also told them that John was speaking about Him (Jesus)!

We do not know how long John was in prison, but his life came to an end in a most evil way. Before he was arrested, John had been speaking against the sin of King Herod because he had taken his brother Philip's wife, who he married. Herod's wife, Herodias, became angry and arranged a plot to trick Herod into killing John. You can read the story in Matthew 14:1-12 and in Mark 6:14-29.

What motivated John to live in the harsh desert, to call

people to turn back to God and to take a stand against both religious and political injustice? The stand that John took led to his death. He was motivated because he knew who Jesus was. Jesus, his relative, was the Son of God! John knew, personally knew, the Son of God.

The comfort we receive from the story of John the Baptist, is that the reality of knowing Jesus empowers us. It causes us to know that our time on earth is like a wisp of smoke compared to the reality of being with God for Eternity. Not many are called to become a martyr as John was. But for those who are, there is glorious grace given to them that they would willingly die for Jesus' sake.

In the book of Acts we see Stephen who, like John, gave his life because he knew Jesus. As he was being killed he looked up and said, "Look, I see heaven open and [Jesus] standing at the right hand of God." Acts 7:56

For both Stephen and John, the key to their ability to remain faithful in spite of the threat of death was Jesus. They knew Jesus. Father God, help us all to know Jesus!

12 - PAUL AND SILAS

When Jesus started his public ministry of preaching and teaching, healing the sick, and working miracles, He chose twelve men to be His close followers, His twelve disciples. In the book of Acts they were known as the Apostles, meaning that they had been chosen by God to go to other places and preach the Good News about Jesus. They had also been given power from God to perform miracles and to be spokesmen on Jesus' behalf.

In the New Testament Paul is also called an Apostle. Before he became an Apostle he was known in the early Church as an enemy and a persecutor of Christians! "Meanwhile, Saul (Paul's name before his conversion) was still breathing out murderous threats against the Lord's disciples." Acts 9:1 This verse in Acts is the beginning of the amazing story of Paul's conversion to Christianity. You may like to read all of Acts 9 for the rest of the story.

In his lifetime Paul wrote many letters to the young churches. These letters make up much of the New Testament. Paul also went on four major missionary journeys, traveling from Jerusalem to Greece and Macedonia. He even sailed to Rome on two different occasions. In Paul's travels he was misused, beaten, and imprisoned several times. His crime was preaching about Jesus. Paul was imprisoned in Rome both times he traveled there and was eventually executed while in Rome. The prisons and jails at the time Paul lived were harsh places where prisoners were deprived of every human comfort and often died in captivity.

Some of the original apostles and other people who had become believers in Christ also went on missionary trips. One of the newer Christians was a man named Silas. He went with Paul on his second journey. See Acts chapters 15-18 for details of Paul and Silas' journey. In the city of Philippi, Paul and Silas were arrested for delivering a slave girl from an evil spirit (Acts 16:16-24). They were severely beaten and put in stocks in an inner cell (Max !) in prison.

Paul and Silas' response to this cruel treatment was to pray and sing hymns to God, **out loud**. The text says that the other prisoners were listening to them (Acts 16:25). God then sent an earthquake that shook the foundations of the prison and freed every prisoner from their shackles and from their cells. God released them all, and then another very unusual thing happened! (You may want to read the rest of the story in Acts 16:25-40.)

I have a lot to learn from Paul and Silas! Complaining over even small annoyances comes very easily to me! But not to Paul and Silas: they prayed and praised God - loudly! The Spirit of God within them enabled them to do a very powerful thing: they rejoiced and praised God, and the Comforter caused an earthquake in the prison! It takes a mighty Spirit to prevent bitter complaint, and instead to cause praise to come from the lips of suffering believers. And that Spirit lives in us if we believe the Gospel. The love of God so captured Paul's soul that he had declared himself "a prisoner for the Lord." Eph. 4:1

Paul certainly has plenty that he could have complained about. He was mistreated and falsely accused, not only by government officials, but also by people within the Church. In Paul's second letter to the Church in Corinth he writes a response to some false apostles who spread lies about him.

"Are they servants of Christ? (I am out of my mind to talk like this.) I am more. I have worked harder, been in prison more frequently, been flogged more severely, and been exposed to death again and again. Five times I received from the Jews forty lashes minus one. Three times I was beaten with rods, once I was stoned, three times I was shipwrecked, I spent a night and a day in the open sea, I have been constantly on the move. I have been in danger from rivers, in danger from bandits, in danger from my own countrymen, in danger from Gentiles; in danger in the city, in danger in the country, in danger at sea; and in danger from false brothers. I have labored and toiled and gone without sleep; I have known hunger and thirst and have gone without food; I have been cold and naked. Besides everything else, I face daily the pressure of my concern for all the churches. Who is weak and I do not feel weak? Who is led into sin and I do not inwardly burn?

If I must boast, I will boast of the things that show my weakness. The God and Father of the Lord Jesus, who is to be praised forever, knows that I am not lying. In Damascus (Syria) the governor under King Aretas had the city of Damascenes guarded in order to arrest me. But I was lowered in a basket from a window in the wall and slipped through his hands." II Corinthians 11:23-33

Only through the power of God could any human suffer in the way Paul suffered for spreading the message about salvation through Jesus. Paul was utterly sold out to God and to the love that inspired him! We have access to that same powerful love, though we are not likely to be called to suffer as Paul did.

Throughout the Bible, from the Old Testament prophets to New Testament preachers, people who loved God served Him regardless of the circumstances. Very few of them were well treated, and many faced great difficulties yet remained faithful to God. Paul describes the love that drew him to God and kept him faithful through hardship and suffering. "For I am convinced that neither death nor life, neither angels nor demons, neither the present nor the future, nor any powers, neither height nor depth, or anything else in all creation, will be able to separate us from the love of God that is in Christ Jesus our Lord." Romans 8:38-39

13 - THE EVANGELISTS

In February of 2018, the world famous evangelist, Billy Graham, died at the age of 99 years. He preached to more than 215 million people in more than 185 countries in his lifetime, speaking to more live audiences than anyone in history. He became a spiritual advisor to the U.S. presidents since Harry S. Truman, and was knighted by Queen Elizabeth in 2011. He was widely known as "America's Pastor." In one of his last interviews he was asked what one thing he wanted to say to the people. He replied, "Tell them, God Loves You!"

Another famous American evangelist, who died in April 2011, was David Wilkerson. He began his preaching ministry in the slums of New York City, but became very well known and traveled abroad to preach the Gospel. He founded Times Square Church in 1987. It is presently located at the Mark Hellinger Theatre in New York City. Rev. Wilkerson wrote a book in 1962 titled The Cross and the Switchblade. This book tells the story of his sometimes harrowing experiences with the gangs of NYC.

These are some comments from Rev. Wilkerson telling of his encounter with a notorious gang leader: "Let me give you a powerful example of God's great resurrection love from my own life: In 1958, I went into the Fort Greene projects in Brooklyn, turf of the notorious Mau Mau gang. When I got up to preach, gang members made cat calls, hooting and yelling. After I finished, I went over to speak to the leaders. One of them was Nicky Cruz, who had tried to kill his own brother. I said, Nicky, Jesus loves you. He spat in my face and laughed. Then he cursed me."

David Wilkerson continues, "But Nicky couldn't shake those words: 'Nicky, Jesus loves you.' Those words made their way into the gang leader's heart, and he couldn't escape their power. He thought, 'Who could ever love me?' Yet the Lord came into Nicky's heart - and Nicky finally knew who he was: a beloved son of God. The truth of God's love changed Nicky Cruz's life.

"Years later, after he had become an evangelist himself, Nicky came to visit our ministry in Texas. I asked him what kept him true to Jesus all these years. He said, 'Brother David, you told me once that Jesus loved me. I became convinced of that. So I just started loving Him back. That's what kept me loving and serving Him.'"

These are two very different men, with two very different callings in their lives, but both were evangelists. All their sermons and the examples of their lives said one powerful message: "God Loves You!"

"God IS love!" That is the Gospel in three words.

"How great is the love the Father has lavished on us, that we should be called children of God! And that is what we are!" IJohn 3:1

"We have come to know and have believed the love which God has for us. God is love, and the one who abides in love abides in God, and God abides in him." I John 4:16

"Things which eye has not seen and ear has not heard, and which have not entered the heart of man, all that God has prepared for those who love Him." I Corinthians 2:9

"Neither height, nor depth, nor any other created thing, shall be able to separate us from the love of God, which is in Christ Jesus our Lord." Romans 8:39

"This is how God showed his love among us: He sent his one and only son into the world that we might live through Him." 1 John 4:9

"This is love: not that we loved God, but that He loved us and sent his Son as an atoning sacrifice for our sins." 1 John 4:10

"For God so loved the world that he gave his one and only son, that whoever believes in Him shall not perish but have eternal life." John 3:16

14 - THAT DREAMER

Most of the history of the people of God starts with God's call to Abram (God later changed his name to Abraham). Abram was a descendent of Noah. His father had settled in Haran which is now southern Iraq. God came to Abram in Haran and asked him to leave his home to go to a place God would show him (Genesis 12:1-9). The early history of God making a nation for Himself begins with Abram, his son Isaac, and Isaac's son, Jacob.

Jacob had twelve sons and one daughter. His second youngest son was named Joseph. Joseph became Jacob's favorite son. This prompted jealousy and even hatred in Joseph's older brothers. At a young age God gifted Joseph with dream interpretation. His brothers called him "that dreamer." (The whole story of Joseph is quite a page-turner! Genesis, chapters 37-50, excluding chapter 38).

Joseph was 17 years old when he left his father's home in Canaan. Like other Bible heroes, Joseph was betrayed by jealous people. His jealous brothers took advantage of him and sold him to a caravan of traders on their way to Egypt. While a slave in Egypt Joseph was again betrayed. He was falsely accused and sent to prison where he spent several years.

We don't know a lot about Joseph's years in the Egyptian prison, but the Bible does say this, "But while Joseph was there in the prison the Lord was with him; He showed him kindness and granted him favor in the eyes of the prison warden. So the warden put Joseph in charge of all those held in the prison, and he was made responsible for all that was done there. The warden paid no attention to anything under Joseph's care, because the Lord was with Joseph and gave him success in whatever he did." Genesis 39:22-23

Joseph's gift of interpretation of dreams eventually led to his release from prison. Through a series of events, Joseph was asked to interpret a very troubling dream of the Pharaoh, the king of Egypt. God gave Joseph the meaning of the strange dream. This impressed Pharaoh so much that he put Joseph in charge of the whole land of Egypt as second in command! At the age of 30 years, Joseph entered the service of the Pharaoh, the king of Egypt.

Joseph had suffered a great deal at a young age, but he remained true to God. After 13 years of hardship, he became a ruler of Egypt along with the king!

(NOTE: Joseph does meet up with his brothers again! That is a great read! Gen. chapters 42-50)

"Blessed is the man who does not walk in the counsel of the wicked or stand in the way of sinners or sit in the seat of mockers. But his delight is in the law of the Lord, and on his law he meditates day and night. He is like a tree planted by streams of water, which yields its fruit in season and whose leaf does not whither. Whatever he does prospers. Not so the wicked! They are like chaff that the wind blows away. Therefore the wicked will not stand in the judgment, nor sinners in the assembly of the righteous. For the Lord watches over the way of the righteous, but the way of the wicked will perish." Psalm 1:1-6

15 - THE DEN OF LIONS

In the Bible, the book of Daniel is one of the shorter Old Testament accounts of one of God's prophets. This comparatively short book is packed with danger and intrigue. Daniel in the Lions' Den is one of those stories that excites children and challenges adults.

Daniel was one of the many Israelites exiled to the city of Babylon when Nebuchadnezzar, the king of Babylonia, besieged Jerusalem. The Babylonians took members of the royal family and young, healthy citizens of the city, along with many of the valuable religious articles from the temple, back with them to Babylon: these were the spoils of war. Most of the exiles became servants and slaves of their captors. [note: Babylonia is presently Syria and Iraq]

At first Daniel was confined with the other Israelites, but he excelled in intellect and learning, and was chosen to personally serve in the King's court. The book of Daniel is a condensed version of Daniel's life, but there are some very interesting and terrifying events in these few pages of the Bible.

As time went by, Babylon became even more decadent and corrupt. As punishment for this God allowed Darius, the King of the Medes and Persians, now Iran, to capture Babylon and take over the kingdom. When the rule of Darius began, Daniel was one of three administrators appointed to rule over the whole country. "Now Daniel so distinguished himself among the administrators and other [leaders] by his exceptional qualities that the king planned to set him over the whole kingdom!" Daniel 6:3   Some of the other rulers were jealous of Daniel and searched for information to discredit him.   They could find nothing, "because he was trustworthy and neither corrupt nor negligent." Daniel 6:4

In order to trap Daniel, these jealous rulers talked the king into issuing a law that no one could pray to any other god or man for the next 30 days. King Darius was the only one who could be prayed to or worshipped for that period of time. The punishment for violating the new law was to be thrown into the den of lions. In spite of this law, Daniel continued his habit of praying to God. "Three times a day he got down on his knees and prayed, giving thanks to his God." Daniel 6:10   "When the king heard this he was greatly distressed; he was determined to rescue Daniel and made every effort until sundown to save him." Daniel 6:14   There was no way to rescind the new law, so Daniel was thrown into the lions' den. "The king said to Daniel, 'May your God, whom you serve continually, rescue you.'" Daniel 6:16

The pit of lions was sealed. Daniel was to remain there all night. The king mourned for Daniel throughout the night and could not sleep, but at first light he ran to the lions' den. The first thing the king heard was, "O king, live forever! My

God sent his angels and he shut the mouths of the lions!" Daniel 6:21-22   The king was overjoyed and immediately commanded all of Daniel's accusers and their families to be thrown into the pit!   The Bible says that the lions overpowered them before they reached the floor of the den! (verse 24)

Then a new decree was written by the king that everyone should "fear and reverence the God of Daniel." Daniel 6:26 Reading this whole account is recommended! Daniel 6:1-28

Daniel's stay in prison was less than 24 hours, but those who are incarcerated today have access to the comfort from the same God as Daniel had. As King Darius said, "For He is the Living God and He endures forever, His kingdom will not be destroyed, His dominion will never end." Daniel 6:26

16 - TIM'S STORY - COMFORT IN CONFINEMENT
by Tim Richard

What started out to be a normal Friday ended up being a most significant day in my life. I had a slight headache and my teeth had hurt for several weeks, but no big deal. My wife told me to call the doctor. So I did and got an afternoon appointment. Nice, I thought, I don't have to wait over the weekend. Because of the doctor's visit and blood work I was told I had leukemia, and ended up in an ambulance headed to The University of Michigan hospital!

When we arrived at the hospital I was told I was in "blast crisis" and could die any moment. That's a very strange thing to be told when you are not expecting it. I went from a normal day, to facing death in a heartbeat. I looked around the room and thought, is this it? Am I done on this earth? Am I really done here? Is this bland room the last thing I'm going to see? I looked over at my wife who was on the other side of the room and thought, "I might not see you for a long time". I silently cried out to God, "I'm out of control, there is nothing I can do, live or die I'm in your hands. I'm trusting you". A peace came over me and from that point on it was like I was watching everything, but from outside myself. It was like a movie - very surreal.

They moved me up to 8-A, the leukemia floor. The rooms were as sterile as they could be. I had my bed, a chair, a window seat and a bathroom. The acute leukemia, or "Cutie Lukie", section of the hospital was extremely clean and only for patients or their guests. Many patients wore masks to protect themselves. With only the aisle way and the patient's room, these tight quarters were very confining, even claustrophobic. By the Grace of God I was able to accept what I was given, and be thankful that I was alive. I was told I had a 20% chance of survival - not good odds. But my wife, as my caregiver, made everything positive, so I was determined to move forward. Attitude is very important for survival.

It's been a year and a half now and I have been in remission for over a year. I did not get to bypass any of the treatments; I went through the "valley of the shadow of death" and very painful times, but I had no fear. I put my trust in God at the very beginning and His love kept all the fear out, and I mean all the fear! "But perfect love drives out all fear." I John 4:18

Can you trust God for your life? I was confined, but I was very free. I was very weak, but He was and is my strength. At times I was alone, but He was with me. I am no different than you; or more or less deserving than you. I did not pick to be in this place, but here I am. And here God gave me grace to choose wisely, to choose the best: "Trust in the Lord with all of your heart and do not lean on your own understanding, in all your ways acknowledge Him and He will direct your paths." Proverbs 3:5   It's all about trusting God; He makes all the difference.

These scriptures are real to me, they gave me the assurance I was going to make it and that I was there for others in the same situation to encourage and strengthen them.

"But now, this is what the Lord says: he who created you, O Jacob, he who formed you, O Israel: 'Fear not, for I have redeemed you; I have summoned you by name; you are mine. When you pass through the waters, I will be with you. When you walk through the fire, you will not be burned; the flames will not set you ablaze. For I am the Lord, your God, the Holy One of Israel, your Savior." Isaiah 43:1-3

"Be anxious for nothing, but by prayer and supplication, with thanksgiving, let your requests be made known to God; and the peace of God, which surpasses all of our understanding, will guard your minds and hearts through Christ Jesus". Philippians 4: 6-7   "I can do all things through Christ who strengthens me". Philippians 4:13

"But if the Spirit of Him who raised Jesus from the dead dwells in you, He who raised Christ from the dead will also give life to your mortal bodies through His Spirit who dwells in you". Romans 8:11

"God has not given us a spirit of fear, but of power and of love and of a sound mind". 2 Timothy 1:7

17 - TRUE FREEDOM
by Cathy Richard

We place a high value on freedom. The freedom to choose, the freedom to express ourselves, the freedom to move about and live in safety are all important and good. But sometimes we live in captivity: a prison of walls, or a prison of our own making, an illness or physical limitation, even our responsibilities can make us feel captive at times. Sometimes we find ourselves in a position we never wanted or expected to be in.

True freedom can still be ours because true freedom is an interior state of mind and spirit. Here is a freedom no one or no circumstance can take from us. And so we must first look for freedom within ourselves.

What is holding you captive? Is it patterns of unhealthy and destructive thinking such as self-condemnation, or thinking others are responsible for your happiness, or self pity? Does your behavior enclose you in a prison of loneliness because you push others away out of fear of rejection? This kind of behavior can include harsh speaking, angry outbursts, judging others, using others, failing to forgive or to apologize, lying and even laziness. We can also become captive to our feelings: fear, anger and resentment, sorrow, and painful memories. These feelings cannot be avoided and are natural but they should not imprison us. We need to learn how to handle feelings in healthy ways or to let them go. Feelings are temporary by nature and should not control or define us.

Our experiences and what we have learned, especially in our childhood, affect us in very deep ways. Recovering from negative occurrences requires a great deal of work on our part and usually help from others. But do not despair, for "all things are possible with God." Mark 10:27   Change, healing and true freedom are within your reach. When you reach out for help with a genuine desire to change and to be free, God Himself will take your hand. And so will others. Hand in hand we hold each other up and walk this journey to true freedom together.

Lately, my own personal "jailer" has been fear. When my husband of 37 years was diagnosed with acute myloid leukemia in Nov. 2016, our lives and our world changed. We had every form of help possible: excellent medical care, two of my husband's brothers matched for the needed stem cell transplant, family and friends provided everything we needed and more; including so much love and prayer! Still, the stress and anxiety were overwhelming at times and all I could do was repeat to myself over and over, "Keep your eyes on Jesus."

All was going well until about 6 months after the transplant when graft vs. host disease came back and caused all sorts of havoc. At one point the doctor mused to himself, yet out loud, that he wondered if the leukemia might be coming back. Fear, a gut wrenching, mind torturing, paralyzing fear, became my constant companion for 6 weeks. Finally my husband's blood work showed improvement and the doctor felt that all would be well.

Of course, we were all greatly relieved. But the year of stress and fear had taken it's toll on my mind, body and spirit. I suffered a mild form of PTSD, post-traumatic stress disorder. I first had to recognize what was going on with me, and then I had to take steps to deal with it. These steps included talking with friends about it, slowing down and being good to myself, starting to exercise again, practicing mindfulness and meditation, and spending a lot of time in prayer.

These may be some steps toward your own freedom: 1. Figure out what is truly holding you captive – this takes some deep soul searching and may take some time to work through the layers. 2. Talk with another person you can trust about it and be honest. 3. Take concrete and realistic steps toward healing and change. Ask for help to identify what these might be. 4. Read the Bible, even if you are not a Christian, or even if you are an atheist. It contains great wisdom for life, assurance that we are loved, and healing for our souls.

Start today, now. Walk to a window or go outside to let the beauty of nature bring you a smile. Smile often, even if you don't feel like it. Sit or stand quietly and focus on your breathing. Say a short prayer: "help me, Jesus" works just fine. Do a kindness, no matter how small, for someone else. Be thankful for every little thing. And I do mean EVERY little (or big) thing - that cute little squirrel in the tree, and the sound of birds singing, a glass of water, a bit of food, your toothbrush, walking, and that you are capable of loving. Never forget that. God has given us the power and the freedom to love: to love God, to love yourself, and to love others. And never forget or refuse to believe that you are loveable and that you are loved. Freedom can be yours. Wherever you are, whatever your past or present, whatever your circumstances, you can be free. You may sometimes feel confined (restricted, lonely, fearful, confused, uncertain or sad), and that's okay. Just don't allow your feelings and thoughts to become your prison. The choice is yours. Little by little, one day at a time, through God we can all live in freedom.

During this process of learning to live free we are in great need of comfort as it is not an easy journey. We all seek comfort during difficult times, but often we chose to find comfort in unhealthy ways – overeating or poor eating choices, unhealthy relationships, alcohol and drugs, or sex. Often it is more than one of these things! These might bring very fleeting, temporary comfort but end up making things worse for us. I find myself skipping exercise and stretching – the very things that would help me to relax and be healthier!

Our most important source of comfort comes from God, Jesus, and the Holy Spirit. And it's free! No guilt, no bad consequences, no regrets. The Bible is the best source of comfort and wisdom. I like to read the Psalms. They are often about suffering people looking for relief and comfort. When I read the Gospels I learn from Jesus about God's love for us, his mercy, forgiveness and grace. I read the letters of the New Testament and find there instruction on how to live in peace and joy, and I can relate to the lives and struggles of others who are trying to live a worthwhile and happy life.

I read the Scriptures every day, morning and night. I read other helpful meditations such as the beautiful little book, "Jesus Calling". God Himself comforts us because we are His precious children! And I need all the help, comfort, guidance and reassurance I can get! One of my favorite Scriptures is "Be still and know that I am God." Psalm 46:10 It reminds me to still myself and to trust in God.

God has given us other resources besides his Word. He gave us community – we were never meant to go it alone in this life and church is a good place to find a caring community; but I have to take the initiative to reach out and get involved. God also gave us this beautiful world we live in. I like to go for walks and listen to the birds sing, notice the light, the patterns and colors, look for beauty in the simplest things and smile. I also like to just stand in front of a window, breathe deeply and slowly and listen for God's

voice in my heart. We can find comfort in healthy ways -
true comfort.

Captivity comes in many forms. Comfort and freedom
comes from the One who made us, loves us and redeems us.
He has promised to never leave or forsake us, and that He
will be with us always. "In all these things we are more than
conquerors through him who loved us." Romans 8:37

18 - I DOUBT THAT

"Doubting Thomas" was a real person and his name has become a label for a person who finds it hard to believe the truth. Thomas, one of Jesus' twelve disciples, has actually earned himself a place in Webster's Dictionary as "Doubting Thomas." The meaning listed there is: "a person who habitually doubts or questions, or a chronic skeptic." This nick-name given to Thomas is perhaps a bit unfair because he was also known as a man capable of devotion and courage, as when he heard that his friend Lazarus had died. (John 11:16) Thomas was the disciple who asked the question of Jesus that prompted one of the best answers in the Bible to the mystery of who Jesus is: "Jesus answered, 'I am the way, the truth, and the life. No one comes to the Father except through me.'" John 14:6

The Bible account of Thomas in which he doubts the resurrection of Jesus is found in John 20:24-29: "Now Thomas, one of the Twelve, was not with the other disciple when Jesus came [to them]. So the other disciples told him, 'We have seen the Lord!' But he said to them, 'Unless I see the nail marks in his hands and put my finger in his side, I will not believe it.' A week later his disciples were in the house again, and Thomas was with them. Though the doors were locked, Jesus came and stood among them and said, 'Peace be with you!' Then he said to Thomas, 'Put your finger here; see my hands. Reach out your hand and put it into my side. Stop doubting and believe.' Thomas said, 'My Lord and my God!' Then Jesus told him, 'Because you have seen me, you have believed; blessed are those who have not seen and yet believed.'"

I imagine that Thomas's joy in seeing Jesus far outweighed the hurt he may have felt at Jesus' response to his unbelief. It was not many days after Jesus appeared to the disciples that He met with them again, and told them this: "Do not leave Jerusalem, but wait for the gift my Father promised... in a few days you will be baptized with the Holy Spirit." Acts 1:4-5   This command was given to them ten days before Pentecost, at which time the promise was fulfilled. Thomas, along with the other disciples, faithfully obeyed Jesus' instructions.

The last time they met together was soon after Jesus had told them to wait in Jerusalem. It was the last time they would see Him on the earth: "...he was taken up before their very eyes, and a cloud hid Him from their sight." Acts 1:9   The time for Him to return to Heaven had come but He promised He would return again (Acts 1:11).   There is no doubt that Thomas faithfully followed Jesus the rest of his life.

The weapons of doubt and unbelief are persistent tactics our enemy, Satan, uses to derail us from receiving the saving grace God wants to give us through belief in Jesus Christ. In The Daily Study Bible, (the Gospel of John), by

William Barclay, are some words about Thomas to encourage us in the battle with doubt and unbelief:

> "Thomas had two great virtues. He absolutely refused to say that he believed when he did not believe...there is an uncompromising honesty about Thomas...he would not pretend that [his doubt] did not exist. Thomas' other great virtue was that when he was sure, he went the whole way! 'My Lord and my God!' said Thomas."
> William Barclay

Be encouraged in the "good fight of faith". Thomas came to faith in the resurrection of Jesus Christ in a harder way than the other disciples came. But through his honest battle with doubt he became a believer! Take comfort: the irresistible grace of God is more powerful than any doubt Satan throws in our way.

The Apostle Paul said to his young friend, Timothy, "Fight the good fight of faith. Take hold of the eternal life to which you were called..." 1 Timothy 6:12   Our best weapon in the fight of faith is God's word - the Bible. Hebrews 4:12 tells us, "For the word of God is full of life and power." Talk to God (pray), read his "living words" and you will win the battle with doubt and unbelief.

> "You will pray to him and he will hear you." Job 22:27

"Ask, and you will be given what you ask for. Seek, and you will find. Knock and the door will be opened. For everyone who asks, receives. Anyone who seeks, finds. If only you will knock, the door will open." Matthew 7:7-8 The Living Bible

19 - HOLLY'S STORY
(anonymous)

I am writing my story as I sit here in prison. God has given me the courage to write this, hoping that it gives hope to someone else. I've been where you are and it feels like the chair got kicked out from under me. But I want to say that there is light in the darkness.

I suppose I came from a home that appeared to be a typical family: Mom & Dad, two girls and a boy. That is where the "typical" part ends. My father was very controlling, negative and critical. As a child and teenager I was not shown love, praise or encouragement. My mom tried to be there for me; but she didn't know how to relate to me, and I pushed her away. She was a Christian but was not able to connect with me.

In my early teen years my family started attending church, but that did not last long. However, my dad made me attend confirmation classes (my siblings did not have to go). I became resentful and was hurting and started to believe the mistaken idea that sex was "love", but that just made the pain worse. I started to rebel. I wanted my parents to hurt like I was hurting. I began lying and stealing money from them. I isolated myself from my family and just listened to music. I did have a relationship with my grandfather; but when he died unexpectedly, I turned my anger toward God. I felt like He had taken away the one person that loved me. I was undone: lost, guilty, angry, and sad. I continued in my sinful ways.

At age sixteen I got a job but my father controlled my money, so after graduating from high school I left home. That wasn't working well, so I returned home after 3 months. At that time I had a boyfriend whom I thought would be a way out of my unhappiness. This turned out to be a very unhealthy relationship because of domestic violence and emotional abuse. I stayed with him because my father despised him! I started getting in trouble with the law and ran up credit card debt and dropped out of college. I was living a destructive life and eventually returned home when the physical abuse was too much.

Returning home was not helpful as nothing had really changed. I had become greedy for money and possessions and had a fear of going without things, so I had major financial problems. My dad had not changed either, so again I looked for a way out. I would not turn to God because of my anger over my grandfather's death. I was a sinner and I knew it: an adulterer, a murderer (I had an abortion), and I was pregnant again. Things went from bad to worse. I married an alcoholic drug addict, so I entered the drug scene to make him happy! I lost who I was and what I wanted to be, and continued to fail at life: college, friendships, and my dreams.

I had one thing in my life that I wanted very much: a

daughter! I believed I was a success at being a mom. I did love my daughter and wanted to stop my life of crime, but I ignored my conscience and sold my soul to the devil. I believed I was in too deep to quit. Greed and false pride ruled my life.

But God in His mercy, rescued me from the snare of destruction I was building. I got arrested! Sitting in the jail, I knew I was a sinner: a thief, a liar, a manipulator, a murderer and an adulterer. I was prideful, but also very fearful, angry, faithless, devastated and extremely worried about my daughter. My world crashed!

In jail I heard a voice telling me over and over to pray. So I did. I felt something break in me! About that time I started getting visits from one of the Jail Ministry workers, a blessing in my life that I am very thankful for. I received a Bible which I began to read but wasn't sure I believed. I was plagued by doubt. Soon, on my sentencing day, I learned I was going to prison. That was the verdict that not one individual in the courtroom, except the judge, thought I would get. Obviously, God had a plan, and prison was part of it.

Not long after arriving in prison I was able to attend a "Kyrex weekend", and I gave my life over to Christ. Then my healing began. I was able to let go of past resentments and forgive those who had hurt me. Since that week-end, I have grown so much spiritually. I am blessed and thankful to be in prison. Yes, I said blessed and thankful! My daughter has formed a deeper bond with her father , my father and I are getting closer; that is taking a lot on my part but God is helping me to forgive him. I've been delivered from the chains of my past. I have new goals, ambitions, and motives. I am no longer a thief, liar, addict, manipulator...etc. But I am still a sinner and need Him every day.

I believe God had to get me away from all the distractions so I could get to know Him. I was powerless to "save" myself, but now I depend on Him. I have learned to talk to God. I say simple prayers to Him all day long. If I am tested, I just say, "Help me, Jesus."

If you don't know God, He is waiting for you, and He has the power to forgive you and help you. God is continually working in me and through me. I am not a perfect Christian. I still sin, but God knows my shortcomings and weaknesses, and He still chose me. (John 15:16 "you did not choose me, but I chose you..."). And He's choosing you - look around at where you are. He has intervened so you can say "yes" to Him and be saved. God is love, and He loves you!   Holly

"And we know that all things work together for good to those who love God, to those who are called to His purpose." Romans 8:28

20 - FEAR NOT

Many places in the Bible we find these two little words: "fear not." Some of the time these words are spoken to people by angels, as when Gabriel announced to Mary that she would give birth to Jesus (Luke 1:26-31). An angel of the Lord appeared to Joseph also to tell him not to be afraid to take Mary as his wife (Matthew 1:18-21). And we all know about the multitude of angels appearing to the shepherds when Jesus was born. The first words the angel spoke were, "Fear not!" Luke 2:8-14

Prior to these angelic appearances an angel had also visited Zechariah the priest with the words "Fear not," announcing to him that he and his wife would have a son in their old age. This son was later known as John the Baptist.

God used angels to speak these encouraging little words to the first New Testament missionaries who found themselves in dangerous or hostile situations. On one of the Apostle Paul's voyages to Rome, God sent an angel to tell him to "fear not" and to give comfort and direction to Paul and those with him. They were adrift in a fierce storm in the Adriatic Sea near Italy and were about to be shipwrecked. But all of those on the ship made it safely to shore (Acts 27).

On another occasion all the apostles who were in Jerusalem had been arrested and put in jail. "During the night an angel of the Lord opened the doors of the jail and brought them out. 'Go stand in the temple courts,' he said, 'and tell the people the full message of this new life.'" Acts 5:17-20

In Jesus' three years of ministry He often said, "Fear not" to his disciples, to individuals, and to groups of people. One of my favorite occurrences is in Luke 12:32 "Fear not, little flock; for it is your Father's good pleasure to give you the kingdom." Jesus said this to reassure the people that God knew all about their physical needs in life and would take care of these things.

Some of our favorite Old Testament Bible stories involve angels. God sent them with the same message, "Fear not." David often wrote in the Psalms of angels who would assist God's people. Psalm 68:17, KJV says, "The chariots of God *are* twenty thousands, *even* thousands of angels." In one of my favorite Psalms David says, "For he shall give his angels charge over thee to keep thee in all thy ways." Psalm 91:11 KJV

The primary way that God spoke to the people in Old Testament times was through the prophets who repeatedly said to the people "fear not." Usually the prophets spoke to the people when they were severely disobeying God's laws and getting into trouble. He sent them to warn the people of impending battles with enemy nations. Often the prophets spoke to those who had already been exiled by their enemies. The message of the prophets was to tell the people to turn back to God and he would help them.

Very often God's prophets were ridiculed and mistreated. The people did not want to be told of their sins. And they certainly did not want to repent, to turn away from sin and follow God's ways. But the prophets loved God and they loved their countrymen. They continued to give God's message of love and forgiveness to the wayward Israelites. Their messages included the words, "fear not," but turn back to God.

In all of the Bible God speaks to reassure the people that they do not need to fear evil in the many forms that it presents itself. However, there is a "fear" that is healthy and good, and necessary. Proverbs 1:7 says, "The fear of the Lord is the beginning of knowledge...". The Living Bible states it this way: "How does a man become wise? The first step is to trust and reverence the Lord." Trust and reverence is the **fear of the Lord**. This is holy fear.

According to The New Bible Dictionary, Tyndale, "Holy fear is God-given, enabling men to have high regard and great respect for God, obeying His commandments and hating evil. In the New Testament emphasis is laid on God as loving and forgiving, the One who through Christ gives men the spirit of sonship and enables them boldly to face up to life and death without fear. Godly fear stimulates the believer to seek holiness, and is reflected in his attitude towards his fellow believers."

"For God hath not given us the spirit of fear; but of power, and of love, and of a sound mind." 11 Timothy 1:7 KJV

"I, even I, am He who comforts you. Who are you that you fear mortal men, the sons of men..." Isaiah 51:12

Since I have mentioned angels several times in this section, I would like to recommend to you a book about angels. The title of the book is, **ANGELS... ringing assurance that we are not alone**. "Yes, angels are real. They are not the product of your imagination. If we had spiritual eyes we would see not only a world filled with evil spirits and powers - but also powerful angels with drawn swords, set for our defense."
- Billy Graham

"Dr. Graham lifts the veil between the visible and invisible world to give us an eye-opening account of these behind-the-scenes agents. This best-selling classic, records the experiences of Dr. Graham and others who are convinced that at moments of special need they have been attended by angels. With keen insight and conviction, Dr. Graham affirms that:

+ God's invisible hosts are better organized than any of the armies of man - or Satan.

+ Angels "think, feel, will, and display emotions."

+ Angels guide, comfort, and provide for people in the midst of suffering and persecution.

+ At death, the faithful will be ushered by angels into the presence of God."

ANGELS was written by Billy Graham in 1975, and republished in 1986, 1994 and 1995.

21 - WAIT...AND PRAY
by Indira Oskvarek

One of the most precious treasures that I have safely kept for over 30 years is a letter from my father. This letter was written to me in 1986 in response to my letter to him about my emotional struggles, frustrations, and inner turmoil in deciding my future career. I had finished my Ph.D. in Biochemistry from a medical institute in India, and was now faced with a process of applying for jobs in my field, or applying for a post-doctoral fellowship in the USA. Other options included joining non-scientific organizations such as working with Mother Teresa to help the poor. And there were also opportunities to do some things totally different. After contemplating all these options, I dropped them! What if I would have to serve others in humility, live an ordinary life, follow rules, have no salary or financial gain, and lose my independence? (Did I have some things to learn!)

My father wrote back sympathizing with my situation. He told me that he and my mother were praying and that I should not worry. His simple advice was to "wait and pray" for God to open the right door. He went on to say, "Just as Jesus told his frightened and worried disciples in the upper room to wait until they received power from above, you too wait. The disciples waited and prayed as Jesus commanded them, and at Pentecost they received the promised gift of the Holy Spirit to empower them. The doors for preaching were then opened (Acts 1:4-5, 2:1-4, 7-8)." My door opened with an opportunity for a position in one of the best institutes in India, and eventually I made my way to the USA, where I still had to wait.

As for many, waiting is still a challenge for me. Patience and trust are still not my best buddies. In the moments of wondering what I was to do, my father's advice, "wait and pray," still echoed in my mind, even after his death twenty-six years ago. We all have gone through periods of waiting in our lives. Our patience has been tested through difficulties, seemingly unanswered prayers, and through holding on in faith. Our preference, of course, would be to live in a less problematic way; to have obstacles removed from our paths without much struggle, to have our prayers answered without delay, and to get what we have asked for.

We all have gone through some difficult and unexpected twists and turns in our lives accompanied by varying periods of waiting. However, the "waiting" has often resulted in much needed growth and maturity in the areas of our lives that were weak and needed to be strengthened in knowledge of God, in character, and in virtues. I Peter 1:3-8, verse seven says..."These have come so that your faith - of greater worth than gold, which perishes even though refined by fire - may be proved genuine and may result in praise, glory, and honor when Jesus Christ is revealed."

When we think about it objectively, waiting is normal in life. We can see this with many examples in nature. Expectant parents must wait for nine months to hold their precious baby. A farmer has to wait to see the fruit of his labor. The crop may take a long time to mature after planting the seed in the ground. The seed cannot be planted one day and its fruit ready to eat the next day. In all these natural processes, waiting is not only required but essential to the desired outcome. Thus, we can justify waiting when it comes to nature.

But think of it, even God who controls all things, had to wait for the appointed time in history to send his Son into the world. And Jesus had to wait thirty-three years to start His earthly ministry. Had we been there to hear Jesus at age twelve debating with the teachers and scholars of the law in the temple for three days (Luke 2:46-47), or after His baptism in Jordan River when the Holy Spirit came down upon him like a dove and a voice came from heaven confirming him as a "beloved Son," we would likely have thought he was ready to start His ministry. No, He had to wait for His appointed time. And that was still not clear when he turned water into wine at the wedding in Cana (John 2: 3-4). It gives us comfort to see that even God had no easy shortcuts but had to wait, and our Lord Jesus also had to wait.

We usually don't understand reasons for waiting, but if we

trust God who knows all things: the beginning, the end, and everything in between, we can begin to relax and trust Him in the times of waiting. The period of waiting can be a difficult time of emotional and spiritual challenge. But it is also a time for growth; to learn, to trust, to develop intimacy with God and to cultivate a deeper relationship with Him. God is also doing the work of breaking and molding us into his desired vessels so we can be more fruitful and used according to His plans and purposes. This involves spiritual pruning which can be painful. He wants to bring out our full potential as His sons and daughters. Even though the outcome sounds wonderful and we think we will show maturity when it comes to a period of waiting again. No! Often we still have more to learn.

I did end up coming to the USA and worked on a post-doctoral project for three years. Then God arranged for me to meet a fine man whom I married. We moved to his small home town. My title changed from research scientist to house wife. After a few months of excitement, I was pushed into the "wait" mode again from 1996-2006, and was again wondering what to do with my life. The answer didn't come easily but I knew I had to work in the area of "serving." I was to start by serving my husband, then the community of which I was going to be a part, and serving God where I was. I didn't take my waiting very gracefully but God was patient with me. I first became a volunteer in various projects for about ten years. For me this was mostly to pass time. I was feeling pretty empty and unproductive which became a very depressing feeling. I was weary, anxious, and frustrated. My complaint was, "Why did God bring me to this small town where I feel like a big zero". I would cry and pray to God wondering if He was looking down on this "big zero." I asked Him to show me clearly His plans. To me God seemed amused and quiet, but I am sure, had He shown me His plan, I would have straightway said "no." How little I knew that He was silently working out His plan while I could see nothing happening in my life for 10 years.

In 2006, to my big surprise, the non-profit charity, Global Compassion Inc., was born out of my long "waiting." It was through the Holy Spirit, but I didn't jump with excitement because God was pushing me into more humility: asking people for money! He slowly kept breaking me and molding me to be a servant. It got easier with years, and now the charity has been serving many poor people in my home country, India, and other poor countries in the world. What God has been doing through me is far bigger and better than what I wanted to do with my limited plans, intellect and education. And as I look back from 2006- 2017, I have personally witnessed in awe, wonder and amazement the magnitude and scope of His plans and purposes unfolding gradually as He tenderly taught me to wait on Him. I know there is more to come. "'For my thoughts are not your thoughts, nor are your ways my ways,' says the Lord. 'For as the heavens are higher than the earth, so are my ways higher than your ways and my thoughts than your thoughts.'" Isaiah 55:8-9

Take heart my friend, if you feel trapped in waiting. God is preparing you for something far bigger than you could ever imagine. "Oh, the depth of the riches of the wisdom and knowledge of God!" Romans 11:33

"But those that wait upon the Lord shall renew their strength: they shall mount up with wings as eagles; they shall run and not be weary; and they shall walk and not faint." Isaiah 40:31 KJV

"Now to Him who is able to do exceedingly abundantly above all we ask or think, according to the power that works in us, to Him be the glory in Christ Jesus!" Ephesians 3:20-21

22 - CLAIR'S STORY
(anonymous)

My journey to Christ began when I was arrested at a young age and sentenced to life in prison. I remember my awareness at the time that I was not mad at God because I knew that he had given me "free will" to determine the right path for my own life. I was just too rebellious to choose the way that would have been best for me. I remember my rejection of God very vividly: I told myself that I was too young to surrender my all to God. But life had a way of turning things around so I could see more clearly!

In the New Testament book of Romans it says, "And we know that in all things God works for the good of those who love him, who have been called according to his purpose." Romans 8:28   Now I can say that I am one of those who are called according to His purpose! All Glory to God!

After my arrest, I was initially offered a plea of 10 years in prison. For reasons that I did not understand, God did not allow the plea agreement to go through. He knew what was best for me, and was much more interested in my eternal destiny that in my immediate happiness.

It took eight years in prison for me to fully surrender my life to my Savior, Jesus Christ. I had become weary of doing things my own way, so I gave myself to Christ and accepted his gift of Salvation in 1999. I was baptized in 2001.

My new life in Christ was not free of hardship. I endured numerous tests; passed some and failed many. I started to read the Bible, from beginning to end. God gave me a burning passion and desire to learn of Him, and to have an intimate relationship with Him: to know God the Father, God the Son, and God the Holy Spirit.

I spent hours reading and studying the Word of God every day. The Holy Spirit opened my mind and heart to God, and I couldn't get enough! God gave me dreams and visions and he showed me His purpose for me on this earth. He led me to take correspondence courses with International Christian College and Seminary. Through a fellow Christian inmate, I was connected to a ministry/charity that helped pay for my schooling.

I have achieved Associate's and Bachelor's degrees in Pastoral Ministry and am currently working on my Master's degree. I give God all the Glory for what He is doing in my life and for providing those on the outside to help me.

The journey has been a long one but here I am, twenty-six years later, trusting God for my release from prison. (I am reminded that Abraham waited 25 years to receive what God has promised to Him.) Now I am going to receive what I have been asking God for. My motion for parole is pending and I believe that the God I serve is able to deliver me out of prison. Expecting release from prison is not the reason I serve God. I serve Him because I have grown to love and respect Him. It is all about Him! No matter where I am I will still serve Him. My treasure is in Heaven, and that is where my heart is also, in Jesus Christ (Matthew 6:19-21).

"But our citizenship is in heaven. And we eagerly await a Savior from there, the Lord Jesus Christ." Philippians 3:21

23 - FORGIVENESS
by Anne Vincenza

In the Bible Jesus tells us to forgive others when they trespass against us, even if they don't acknowledge their wrong or ask to be forgiven. Forgiving comes with time as we ask God to help us forgive daily and for our hearts to match our words. We can be encouraged by knowing that God never asks us to do something He won't help us do.

I John 1:9 is very simple: "If we confess our sins he is faithful and just and will forgive us our sins and purify us from all unrighteousness." The reason God forgives us is that Jesus Christ paid the price for our sins by dying in our place. When we trust Him as our Savior, he forgives us. It is not only our sin he forgives but also our stupidity.

Even though we are forgiven, it is often very difficult to let go of our feelings of guilt. Sometimes when we feel very guilty we come to believe that this feeling is actually our punishment. We must trust God to free us from guilt. Jesus died for our sin and guilt. We need not carry it around with us.

When I went to prison, I had two young children, ages five and three. This provided many reasons to feel tremendous guilt because I was not there for birthdays, special events, sickness, and all the times they cried for me.

My grandparents raised me and were always "there" for me and now I am not there for them. When my mother became ill my children were devastated. Yet again I was not there. The list goes on and on. I was in an endless cycle of repetitive torment, believing that the pain of guilt was somehow good for me, that I needed to live in the pain of my wrong decisions.

The pattern of guilt can be never ending and destructive if we don't let God help us change it. I cannot change the past but I can get out of the cycle of guilt: the "if not for this I would be there" or "I would not have missed out." This kind of thinking only leads to being stuck in the same place, not being able to move forward.

I have learned to focus on things I do have control over, be supportive to my loved ones, change my attitudes, and set goals to keep moving forward. Yes, I messed up, but I don't have to keep messing up.

Accepting grace and mercy from God for what brought me here has helped me know His forgiveness. "No longer will a man teach his neighbor, or a man his brother, saying, 'Know the Lord,' because they will all know me, from the least to the greatest, declares the Lord. For I will forgive their wickedness and remember their sin no more." Jeremiah 3:34

Forgiveness is a gift I have given myself, as I have received grace and mercy from God. I can also extend grace and mercy to others. I am still reminded of my guilt, but I can dwell on His mercies that are new every day. Never give up on yourself, learn from your mistakes, and try again. Tomorrow is right around the corner. Straighten your crown and remember whose you are. God has forgiven you. Forgive yourself and others, and they will forgive you, too.

"The Lord's lovingkindnesses indeed never cease. For his compassions never fail. They are new every morning; Great is thy faithfulness." Lamentations 3:22-23

24 - MY JOURNEY THROUGH ANXIETY AND DEPRESSION
by Susan Rademacher

Growing up, I had a very privileged childhood. I was blessed with wonderful parents, a beautiful home, cars, all modern comforts, an excellent education, and faith and church community. To top it off, we were referred to as "the country club" people, meaning we were well off. So, one might wonder how come someone like me could end up falling to the depth of hell, wanting only to kill myself?

As I look back, there was mostly one reason. I had not been properly taught how to deal with unpleasant emotions. I was the "fat kid" and was mercilessly teased by my peers, siblings and even by my parents. Those were the most painful, emotionally humiliating, shameful and heartbreaking memories of my childhood in spite of all the comforts that surrounded me. Those memories still haunt me sometimes and it still hurts deeply. It was because I didn't have any trusted person to confide in about my hurt feelings and heartaches, that I turned inward and isolated myself. That only created more emotional turmoil and raging battles in my young mind.

I considered myself unloved and neglected: an unfavorable child. I tried so hard to please my parents, siblings, friends and others, that it created unbearable anxiety. The anxiety caused me to strive even more to please others which created even deeper wounds. As I compared myself with others, I believed that I would never win anyone's approval. Through all my turmoil I learned to hide my emotions so no one would know that I was struggling. I was afraid of becoming a target of even more teasing, laughter, and ridicule if I expressed my feelings. So, I buried my hurt, humiliation and heartaches and put on a "Pollyanna" face. The masquerade worked only for a while.

In my twenties the facade started to crack open which set the stage for my severe anxiety and depression. To make things worse my "best friend" turned out to be the devil incarnate to me. I know now, "the thief comes to steal and to kill and to destroy but Jesus has come so that we may have life and that we may have it more abundantly." John 10:10

Fast forward to my life as an adult. If you were to meet me on the street, you might say that I was friendly, joyful, funny, enthusiastic, compassionate, and sincere. I was also a loyal friend, willing to walk the extra mile for someone in need. I was generous, had high energy and was a hard worker. What you wouldn't know was that I walked on a tightrope every day to stay away from depression and anxiety. Too much stress, lack of sleep and exercise, choosing an unhealthy diet, and having friends who were a bad influence on me caused me to sink deeper into depression and anxiety. I had even driven myself to attempt suicide. I was in a hell-like prison, a debilitating mental disease.

My prison was anxiety and depression. I experienced a wide range of symptoms such as losing interest in things I once took pleasure in. I pulled away socially and hid myself. Deep sadness and despair were my companions. Inability to concentrate, insomnia, fatigue, suicidal thoughts (and attempts), shame, guilt, hopelessness, and over-eating comprised my life.

But I did find comfort and healing in my captivity!

First, I admitted to a healthcare professional that I needed help. The help I received included taking prescribed medication. I soon realized that medication was only part of the fight to regain mental stability. The most important piece of the puzzle was prayer to the "Great Physician" who is God. He is my Lord and Savior, Jesus Christ, who healed so many. Luke 4:40 says, "When the sun was setting, the people brought to Jesus all who had various kinds of sickness, and laying his hands on each one he healed them." I knew my true hope and healing was in Christ. "But he was pierced for our transgressions, he was crushed for our iniquities; the punishment that brought us peace was upon him, and by his wounds we are healed." Isaiah 53: 5

I cried for help and prayed earnestly to God to show me the way out of this misery. I was asking for divine intervention and light in my darkness. By the grace of God, I met and became friends with a Christian woman who invited me to join a very comprehensive Bible study. I could see God listening to my cry and coming to my help through this group. God's word started to work in my life and I started to experience lifting of my burdens. The chains that had held me captive for so many years started to break off. I felt the peace of Christ and his loving arms to hold me. His words, "I am with you," and "do not be afraid," gave me great comfort and relief. I understood who I was in Christ. I learned to pray for protection, which gave me a strong boost of strength and victory.

The lessons I learned along the way:

I understood as a believer that I am constantly engaged in a spiritual warfare (Ephesians 6:12), and I have been equipped through the Word of God to put on the whole armor of God (Ephesians 6:13-18).

Matthew 7:7 says, "Ask and it shall be given to you; seek and you will find; knock and the door will be opened to you." Jesus tells us to be persistent in pursuing God until we get the answers to our prayers that are according to the will of God. God always wants to give good gifts to his children. Healing was at the heart of

Jesus' ministry.

Follow through. After a few half hearted attempts it was easy for me to say that God simply could not be found. It was easy to get discouraged and to want to give up. That's when I surrounded myself with faith-filled friends. I took God sincerely. With deeper faith and commitment, I began to start my day with 30 minutes of quality time one on one with God while the day was new and fresh. This became a time to fix my eyes and heart on Jesus and read his word. I found that this time with God became a determining point that set the tone for my entire day.

I also made a conscious effort to keep my day in God's will and not my own, checking on myself from time to time, and asking the Holy Spirit to lead and guide me. At night before going to bed, I would write in my gratitude journal and contemplate my day, repenting for the times I failed to do right. When I couldn't sleep, I would repeat some verses and pray the Lord's Prayer. Praising and worshipping the Lord kept my mind from taking me somewhere else.

Physical wellness is important. I made it a priority to spend time getting myself in shape. This involved eating healthy foods and getting regular daily exercise. My body is a temple of God, and the Holy Spirit lives within me (1 Corinthians 3:16, 17). It is my responsibility to keep the "temple" clean and not defile it with sinful actions like over eating or eating junk food; and keeping gossip and other toxic thoughts from entering in or going out of my mouth.

Choosing good friends is essential. I surrounded myself with godly women who would be my friends to support me, encourage me, and inspire me to achieve my goals and walk my faith journey.

I rejoice in the Lord as He speaks to me and gladdens my heart (Zephaniah 3:16 and 17). I have learned the great secret weapon to use against the enemy attacks. It is Praise and Worship. "About midnight Paul and Silas were praying and singing hymns to God, and the other prisoners were listening to them." Acts 16:25 "...Jehoshaphat appointed men to sing to the Lord and to praise him for the splendor of his holiness as they went out at the head of the army, saying: : 'Give thanks to the Lord, for his love endures forever.'" 2 Chronicles 20:21-22 Also I find great comfort in reading the Psalms.

I thank God for all his blessings and generously share them with anyone I see in need. This is why I have shared my story: so that you can also find healing and hope in Christ who loves us unconditionally. He paid the price on the cross to bring salvation and healing to us. God bless you!

"On that day they will say to Jerusalem, 'Do not fear, O Zion; do not let your hands hang limp. The Lord your God is with you. He is mighty to save. He will take great delight in you, he will quiet you with his love, he will rejoice over you with singing.'" Zephaniah 3:16-17

25 - PRISON TO PRAISE

The author of the previous testimony mentioned the "great secret weapon" she discovered to use in her battle with Satan. This chapter is about one of the examples from the Bible she uses. Her other example, "Paul and Silas," is in Chapter 12.

A book by the title, Prison to Praise, was written by Merlin Carothers in 1970 and updated in 1983. It was a hugely popular book and spoke truth to many people. In the New Testament the account of Paul and Silas in prison is an example of the power of praise for believers. The Old Testament has a similarly exciting story of the saving and liberating power of praise.

In this story the Kingdom of Israel had become divided into the northern kingdom of Israel and the southern kingdom of Judah. (about 930 B.C.) This division was due to a dispute over who should be the king. Both kingdoms had a series of good and bad kings; good kings who worshipped God, and bad kings who did what seemed right to them. The bad kings led the people of God into idol worship, conforming to the religions of the nations around them.

Most of the kings of Israel were bad; this was the time and place of the very evil King Ahab and his just-as-evil wife Jezebel. The southern kingdom of Judah had many more good kings than bad. They worshipped God and tried to follow His laws.

Most of the prophets in the Old Testament arrived on the scene after both kingdoms had fallen to the Assyrian and Babylonian/Persian empires. The reason God sent the prophets was that the people needed guidance and comfort from Him because of the hard conditions they lived in due to their captivity. Some of the people continued to live in Israel or Judah, and some were exiled to foreign countries.

An Old Testament "prison to praise" occurrence involved one of the good kings in Judah. The name of the king was Jehoshaphat (gee-hos-a-fat). The incident is written in 2 Chronicles 20:1-30. It's a very good read - I recommend it to you!

Upon hearing that Judah would soon be under attack from the Moabites, the Ammonites, and the Meunites (2 Chron. 20:1-2), Jehoshaphat's first thought was to "inquire of the Lord." He proclaimed a "fast," and the people of Judah came together from "every town in Judah" to seek help from God! Jehoshaphat led the people in a faith-filled prayer, asking God for help (2 Chron. 20:6-9). He ended the prayer with these words: "O God, won't you stop them? We have no way to protect ourselves against this mighty army. We don't know what to do, but we are looking to you." 2 Chron. 20:12 The Living Bible   "All the men of Judah, with their wives and children and the little ones, stood before the Lord." (Notice the "Littles!")

After they had prayed, the Spirit of the Lord came upon Jahaziel, the priest. He spoke God's words of encouragement to the king and the people. The message included instructions for them to follow. The priest also said, "You will not have to fight this battle. Take up your positions; stand firm and see the deliverance the Lord will give you, O Judah and Jerusalem. Do not be afraid, do not be discouraged..." (verse 17)

Jehoshaphat and all the people immediately responded with worship to God...with a very loud voice." (v. 18-19) The record of the battle is in verses 20-30. The key to winning this battle was Praise, as it was with Paul and Silas. As they praised God, "the Lord set ambushes against the men of Ammon and Moab and Mt. Seir who were invading Judah, and they were defeated." (v.22)

The reason that "praise to God" is so powerful is that it is an expression of faith (Matthew 17:20 says that faith can remove mountains). When everything looks bleak and life is not going well, praising God is "faith" speaking out loud to God, as well as to our enemy. Praise says, "I love you God, and I trust you with my life." God's response to faith in his people is to act in their behalf. His response may be immediate, or it may come "in due time" according to his wonderful plan for us.

"And we know that in all things God works for the good of those who love him, who have been called according to his purpose." Romans 8:28

Another translation: "Moreover we know that to those who love God, who are called according to his plan, everything that happens fits into a plan for good." Romans 8:28 J. B. Phillips

26 - FREEDOM FROM ANY PRISON
by Susan Thode

My mother wrote the following poem early in the stages of Alzheimer's. My mom was a beautiful and intelligent woman. A Registered Nurse, mother of seven children and a pastor's wife, she sang beautifully and played the piano like a professional. Alzheimer's claimed her in her early fifty's and she became a prisoner of dementia until her death in her 70's. A long time to be in Alzheimer's prison with no hope of parole.

Prisons come in all shapes and sizes, seen and unseen, man-made, self-made, some permanent, some temporary. One thing all prisons have in common is that God offers comfort in any kind of prison and offers freedom in Him from any kind of prison.

My mother did not escape the bodily and mental prison of Alzheimer's until her physical death. But her spirit soared free in Christ her entire life because of her faith in God. Her comfort and freedom came from knowing, "For I am convinced that neither death nor life, neither angels nor demons, neither the present nor the future, nor any powers, neither height nor depth, nor anything else in all creation, will be able to separate us from the love of God that is in Christ Jesus our Lord." Romans 8:38-39

Confusion
Elaine Rex

I'm like a fish out of water,
And like a bird in the sea.
Just can't get things together;
What's the matter with me?

It's still early in the day time
And it seems it should be night,
Things are topsy-turvy
And nothing's going right!

My Father said He'd care for me
And never let me flee—
I know it's not my Father's fault
And so it must be me!

I can't get things together—
Seems I've lost my listening ear;
And still I know my Father's heart:
He said he would be here.

Tomorrow is another day
And maybe the sun will shine
But I can't get things together enough
To even worry about the time!

Time when I should be producing,
Time when I should share—

But I can't get things together enough—
So I'll just leave them in His care!

He spoke to me and said, "Not so!
I've given you some work to do.
People are waiting for you to speak
And tell them I love them , too."

I'm trying to get it together now
And step by step, He'll show me how.
His love spills over from others to me
And that's exactly what He wants from me.

My mother experienced the prison of a tragic chronic health condition for much of her life. Recently I found a scrap of paper in some of her things. Following is a transcription of her handwritten note to herself from 1955.

"From the time I first remember being in Church I was eager to follow the Lord's will in my life and to try to follow in the foot steps of Jesus. I grew considerably through the Christian education programs of our Church, but there is one moment in my life that stands out more than any regarding my growth as a Christian. When my oldest child was 12 years old she became very ill. In spite of prayers and devout intercession, it was very clear to me that Sally did not have very many days to live. I was the hostess for a group of ladies from the church. Sally was feeling poorly and I went to her bedroom to rub her back. I tried to make her as comfortable as I could. As she began to fall asleep I was overcome with the seriousness of her illness, and as I sat on the edge of her bed the tears came. And then I felt a hand on my shoulder and looked around to see if John [Dad] was there. But he wasn't. Then I heard a voice clearly say, 'I am going to take Sally home.'"

I was only four years old when my big sister, Sally, died of bone cancer when she was twelve years old. I don't remember much from that time. What I do remember is my mom's testimony later in life about Sally's death. Mom seemed sad much of the time, but she always said, "The main thing is Sally is not in pain any more. I know I will see her in heaven and that is a joy I look forward to."

God's voice brought my mother a heartbreaking message, but Mom felt at peace knowing Sally would be freed from a prison of agonizing terminal illness. I believe the peace Mom experienced from God's presence in 1955 sustained her through her whole life.

Regardless of the nature of a prison, His presence and peace are available to anyone who will ask.

27 - GOD'S WAR ROOM

Wait a minute! What kind of comfort is war? I just want peace and quiet! I'm tired of fighting battles! I'm tired of bickering, misunderstandings, bad-tempers, betrayals, conflict, anger, hatred, war, pain and death!

Yes, these are all part of the world we live in and part of our human condition. Even nature around us is at war: natural disasters, the battles in the animal kingdom, draught and famine and pestilence. The list goes on. Ever since the first act of disobedience to God in the Garden of Eden, which allowed sin into God's perfect creation and into every human heart, life has been a battle! Running away or pretending that evil doesn't exist are not options. There are no successful pacifists in God's Kingdom!

The "comfort" in life's battles is that God says we can be winners! Specifically, every person can be a winner; and generally, The Kingdom of God wins the battle! "I've read the back of the book, and we win!" is a popular paraphrase of Billy Graham's words, "I've read the last pages of the Bible, it's all going to turn out all right." Of course, the book of Revelation is at the back of The Book, and we do win! This book tells us that there will be a great cosmic and epic battle after Jesus Christ returns to this earth to take all believers to Heaven. This will be a battle that we do not have to fight! When the Mighty Commander and Chief,

Jesus Christ wins the last battle, there is victory for every believer in Him!

"I saw the Holy City, the new Jerusalem coming down out of Heaven from God, prepared as a bride beautifully dressed for her husband. And I heard a loud voice from the throne saying, 'Now the dwelling of God is with men, and He will live with them. He will wipe away every tear from their eyes. There will be no more death or mourning or crying or pain, for the old order of things has passed away.' He who was seated on the throne said, 'I am making all things new!'" Revelation 21:2-5

Following are some words from Psalm 68, a psalm of battle:

"May God arise, may his enemies be scattered; as smoke is blown away by the wind may you blow them away;" v. 1-2

"Sing to God, sing praises to his name, extol him who rides on the clouds..." v. 4

"A father to the fatherless, a defender of widows is God in his holy dwelling. God sets the lonely in families, he leads forth the prisoners with singing, but the rebellious live in a sun-scorched land." v. 5-6

"The chariots of God are tens of thousands and thousands of thousands; the Lord has come from Sinai into his sanctuary." v.17

"Praise be to the Lord, to God our Savior, who daily bears our burdens." v. 19

"Our God is a god who saves; from the Sovereign Lord comes escape from death. Surely God will crush the heads of his enemies," v. 20-21

"Summon your power, O God show us your strength, O God, as you have done before." v. 28

"You are awesome, O God in your sanctuary; the God of Israel gives power and strength to his people. Praise be to God!" v. 35

King David wrote this psalm. He fought in many battles and knew the power of God to save! Hebrews 13:8 says, "Jesus Christ is the same yesterday, today, and forever." This never-changing God loves us and is for us and not against us. He has the power and the authority to rescue us and to help us in the battles of life that we face.

> "The Lord himself goes before you and he will be
> with you; he will never leave you nor forsake you.
> Do not be afraid; do not be discouraged."
> Deuteronomy 31:18

> "Though I am surrounded by troubles, you will
> bring me safely through them. You will clench
> your fist against my angry enemies! Your power
> will save me." Psalm 138:7 TLB

"So do not fear for I am with you; do not be dismayed, for I am your God." Isaiah 41:10

"He shall not be afraid of evil tidings: his heart is fixed, trusting in the Lord." Psalm 112:7 KJV

"The eyes of the Lord are upon the righteous, and his ears are open to their cry." Psalm 34:15

28 - PAUL'S WAR ROOM

Paul's war room really is God's war room, but Paul brings us the message from God to tell us who our enemy is and how we can fight the battle in our lives.

Knowing that we are in a battle that is bigger than ourselves, and too difficult for us to win without God's help, is the first step to victory. We can agree with God that we need Him and cannot make it on our own. There is great power in agreeing with God who is the source of all the power that we need. To agree with God is merely to believe his Word, the Bible.

Paul tells us in the book of Ephesians that our enemy is not other people: "For our struggle is not against flesh and blood, but against the rulers, against the authorities, against the powers of this dark world, and against the spiritual forces of evil in the heavenly realms." Eph. 6:12 Since the battle is not against human beings, we cannot fight this fight using human resources (note from NIV Study Bible).

Paul explains what our spiritual weapons are in Eph. 6:13 "Therefore put on the full armor of God, so that when the day of evil comes, you may be able to stand your ground, and after you have done everything, to stand." Using the picture of a Roman soldier, Paul proceeds to state what these weapons are: "Stand firm then with the belt of truth buckled around your waist, with the breastplate of righteousness in place, and with your feet fitted with the readiness that comes from the gospel of peace. In addition to all this, take the shield of faith, with which you can extinguish all the flaming arrows of the evil one. Take the helmet of salvation and the sword of the Spirit, which is the Word of God. And pray in the Spirit on all occasions with all kinds of prayers and requests. With this in mind, be alert and always keep praying for all the saints." Eph. 6:14-18 (By the way, saints are other Christians.)

My mom who is now in Heaven, had written in her Bible next to Eph. 6:14-18, "PUT ON JESUS!"

Let's look briefly at each piece of armor:

1. Belt of Truth - God's Word is truth. Jesus said, "You will know the truth and the truth will set you free." John 8:32

2. Breastplate of Righteousness - "This righteousness from God comes through faith in Jesus Christ to all who believe." Romans 3:22

3. Shoes of the Gospel of Peace - "How beautiful on the mountains are the feet of those who bring good news, who proclaim peace, who bring good tidings, who proclaim salvation, who say to Zion, 'Your God reigns!'" Isaiah 52:7

4. Shield of Faith - "For everyone born of God overcomes the world. This is the victory that has overcome the world, even our faith." 1 John 5:4

5. Sword of the Spirit - God's Word is the Sword of the Spirit. "For whatever God says to us is full of living power: it is sharper than the sharpest dagger, cutting swift and deep into our innermost thought and desires with all their parts, exposing us for what we really are." Hebrews 4:12 Living Bible

Paul says in Colossians 2:10 "...and you are complete in him, which is the head of all power and authority." We have all we need to fight and win the battles we are engaged in. We can bravely move forward with faith in God, who is our gentle Shepherd who leads and guides us (See Psalm 23).

29 - THE ARMOR OF GOD

Ephesians 6:10-18, gives us a quick review of the power we have in Jesus Christ because of the armor we have available to us. Paul tells us about the battle Christians encounter, and how we can win that battle. Following is Ephesians 6:10-18 in a modern translation.

"A final word: Be strong with the Lord's mighty power. Put on all of God's armor so that you will be able to stand firm against all strategies and tricks of the Devil. For we are not fighting against people made of flesh and blood, but against the evil rulers and authorities of the unseen world, against those mighty powers of darkness who rule this world, and against wicked spirits in the heavenly realms. Use every piece of God's armor to resist the enemy in the time of evil, so that after the battle you will still be standing firm. Stand your ground, putting on the sturdy belt of truth and the body armor of God's righteousness. For shoes put on the peace that comes from the Good News, so that you will be fully prepared. In every battle you will need faith as your shield to stop the fiery arrows aimed at you by Satan. Put on salvation as your helmet, and take the sword of the Spirit, which is the Word of God. Pray at all times and on every occasion in the power of the Holy Spirit. Stay alert and be persistent in your prayers for all Christians everywhere." Ephesians 6:10-18 New Living Translation

The well-known evangelist, David Wilkerson, said this:

"Jesus has the power to purify us. And that power is available to us only as we rest in knowing we are children of God - and that he loves us You may have spent weeks, months, years doing battle with your sin. You may have gritted your teeth and promised both God and yourself, 'I will beat this thing. I will win!' No! Talk to your Father today. Take a look at that life-sucking habit that holds you, and let faith pour out of your heart: Oh, Lord my powerful Savior, I know you love me. And you have all the power I need. I am weak, helpless. But I trust in your power to cast out this evil thing. Lord, I need a miracle of deliverance. You are going to set me free! [If we belong to Jesus] we have a Spirit in us greater than any demon in this world: 1 John 4:4 'You are of God, little children, and have overcome them, because he who is in you is greater than he who is in the world.' His Spirit empowers us in all battles with the flesh and the devil: 'Now to him who is able to do exceedingly abundantly above all we ask or think, according to the power that works in us...'" Ephesians 3:20

(Note: It may be helpful to have a Christian friend pray with you in agreement for the deliverance you need. Jesus said in Matthew 18:19, "I tell you the truth if two of you on earth agree about anything you ask for, it will be done for you by my Father in heaven.")

"See how much our heavenly Father loves us, for he allows

us to be called his children, and we really are! But the people who belong to this world don't know God, so they don't understand that we are his children. Yes, dear friends, we are already God's children, and we can't even imagine what we will be like when Christ returns. But we do know that when he comes we will be like him, for we will see him as he really is. And all who believe this will keep themselves pure, just as Christ is pure." 1 John 3:1-3 New Living Translation

Let's allow this classic hymn to build our faith in victory through Jesus:

Battle Hymn of the Republic
Julia Ward Howe

Mine eyes have seen the glory of the coming of the Lord,
He is trampling out the vintage where the grapes of wrath
    are stored;
He hath loosed the fateful lightning of His terrible swift
    sword,
His truth is marching on.

I have seen Him in the watch-fires of a hundred circling
    camps,
They have builded Him an altar in the evening dews and
    damps;
I can read His righteous sentence by the dim and flaring
    lamps,
His day is marching on.

He has sounded forth the trumpet that shall never
call retreat,
He is sifting out the hearts of men before His
judgment seat;
O be swift, my soul, to answer Him, be jubilant, my
feet!
Our God is marching on.

In the beauty of the lilies Christ was born across the
sea.
With a glory in His being that transfigures you and
me;
As He died to make men holy let us live to make men
free!
While God is marching on.

Chorus

Glory! glory! Hallelujah!
Glory! glory! Hallelujah!
Glory! glory! Hallelujah!
His truth is marching on!

30 - WORDS OF COMFORT FROM ISAIAH

Of all sixteen prophets in the Bible who have books of the Bible named for them, I have found the most words of comfort in the book of Isaiah. Jeremiah also speaks tender words to a hurting people. He is known as the "weeping prophet". Sometimes the prophets were not well treated by the very people they tried to help; but because of their love for God, they wanted to help the people return to Him so He could heal and restore and bless them.

You might want to "adopt" some of these words from Isaiah. They may speak to the needs you have and help build your faith to believe that God wants to help you; He has all the power in Heaven and Earth to do so.

From the Book of Isaiah: (NIV unless stated)

"No matter how deep the stain of your sins, I can take it out and make you as clean as freshly fallen snow." 1:18 The Living Bible

"He will teach us His ways, so that we may walk in his paths." 2:3b

"For to us a child is born, to us a son is given, and the government will be on his shoulders. And he will be called Wonderful Counselor, Mighty God, Everlasting Father, Prince of Peace." 9:6

"You will keep in perfect peace him whose mind is steadfast, because he trusts in you." 26:3

"Whether you turn to the right or to the left, your ears will hear a voice behind you saying, 'This is the way; walk in it.'" 30:21

"The fruit of righteousness will be peace; the effect of righteousness will be quietness and confidence forever." 32:17-18

"...and the ransomed of the Lord will return. They will enter Zion with singing; everlasting joy will crown their heads. Gladness & joy will overtake them." 35:10

"He gives strength to the weary and increases the power of the weak." 40:29

"So do not fear, for I am with you; do not be dismayed, for I am your God. I will strengthen you and help you; I will uphold you with my righteous right hand." 41.10

"For I am the Lord, your God, who takes hold of your right hand and says to you, Do not fear, I will help you." 41:13

"I, the Lord, have called you in righteousness. I will take hold of your hand." 42:6

"I will lead the blind by ways they have not known, along unfamiliar paths I will guide them; I will turn the darkness into light before them and make the rough places smooth.

These are the things I will do; I will not forsake them." 42:16

"When you go through deep waters and great trouble, I will be with you. When you go through rivers of difficulty, you will not drown! When you walk through the fire of oppression, you will not be burned up - the flames will not consume you." 43:2 The Living Bible

"Shout for joy, O heavens; rejoice, O earth: burst into song, O mountains! For the Lord comforts his people and will have compassion on his afflicted ones." 49:13

"Can a mother forget the baby at her breast and have no compassion on the child she has borne? Though she may forget, I will not forget you! See I have engraved you on the palms of my hands." 49:15-16a

"But He was wounded and bruised for our sin. He was chastised that we may have peace; He was lashed-- and we were healed." 53:5 The Living Bible

"We are the ones who strayed away like sheep! We, who left God's paths to follow our own. Yet God laid on HIM the guilt and sins of every one of us!" 53:6 The Living Bible

"O my afflicted people, tempest-tossed and troubled, I will rebuild you on a foundation of sapphires and make the walls of your houses from precious jewels." 54:11

"No weapon forged against you will prevail, and you will

refute every tongue that accuses you. This is the heritage of the servants of the Lord, and this is their vindication from me, declares the Lord." 54:17

"Let the wicked forsake his way and the evil man his thoughts. Let him turn to the Lord, and he will have mercy on him, and to our God, for he will freely pardon." 55:7

"In all their affliction He was afflicted, and He personally saved them. In His love and pity He redeemed them and lifted them up and carried them through all the years." 63:9 The Living Bible

"For since the world began no one has seen or heard of such a God as ours, who works for those who wait for Him." 64:4 The Living Bible

"Before they call I will answer; while they are still speaking I will hear." 65:24

31 - MORE WORDS OF COMFORT

Other prophets brought words of comfort to God's people. Here are a few of those.

Jeremiah cared deeply for God's rebellious people.

"I will give them a heart to know me, that I am the Lord. They will be my people and I will be their God, for they will return to me with all their heart." Jer. 24:7

"For I know the plans I have for you, declares the Lord, plans to prosper you and not to harm you, plans to give you a hope and a future. Then you will call upon me and come and pray to me, and I will listen to you. You will seek me and find me when you seek me with all your heart." Jer. 29:11-13

"But I will restore you to health and heal your wounds, declares the Lord, because you are called an outcast, Zion for whom no one cares." Jer. 30:17

"For long ago the Lord had said to Israel: I have loved you, O my people with an everlasting love; with loving kindness have I drawn you to me." Jer. 31:3

"O Lord God! You have made the heavens and the earth by your great power; nothing is too hard for you." Jer. 32:17

"I will give them one heart and mind to worship me forever,

for their own good and for the good of all their descendants." Jer. 32:39

"Nevertheless, I will bring health and healing; I will heal my people and let them enjoy abundant peace and security." Jer. 33:6

The prophet Hosea said to God's people:

"I led them with cords of human kindness, with ties of love, I lifted the yoke from their neck and bent down to feed them." Hosea 11:4

Ezekiel told them this:

"I will give them an undivided heart and put a new spirit in them: I will remove from them their heart of stone and give them a heart of flesh." Ezekiel 11:19

God is a God of comfort. He longs to comfort you and me. He comes alongside us in our place of captivity to bring comfort, healing and freedom. Read the comforting words of Jesus , of the Old Testament prophets and of the Psalms. Pray those words over yourself and trust that God will act.

While these aren't words of Scripture, we're going to end this devotional with a poem written years ago by my youngest sister. And as we do, I pray, as the apostle Paul prayed, that the eyes of your heart would be enlightened so that you would truly and deeply know the hope that you have in Jesus (Ephesians 1:16-21).

ROBINS IN THE SNOW
by Ruth Dorman

Once through the window I watched
some poor pregnant robins
wading through the snow--

They were so helpless --
victims of circumstance,
unwilling participants
in Nature's mistake.

And I wanted to scream.
I wanted to curse
Winter for staying and
Spring for delaying.
I wanted to melt the snow
by the force of my will.

But the robins believed.
And I remember
when I am struggling through
the frozen wasteland
of unfulfilled promises, carrying the burden
of unborn joy,
I remember the robins
And I believe.

Spring will come.

"Come to a place of safety, all you prisoners, for there is yet hope! I promise right now , I will repay you two mercies for each of your woes."

Zecharaiah 9:12 The Living Bible

Contributors

Ruth Dorman

Rena Henderson

Gerry McIvor

Indira Oskvarek

Susan Rademacher

Cathy Richard

Tim Richard

Susan Thode

Anne Vincenza

Julie grew up as a P.K. (preacher's kid), living with her parents and six siblings. Her father had worked for a time as the chaplain of Montana State Prison. Perhaps this family experience planted seeds of interest in those who lived in captivity, incarcerated and isolated. It was after her five children were raised and gone from home that she first stepped into a jail and heard the door lock behind her. This led to ten years in jail ministry, teaching, and speaking encouragement to many women. She says that part of her heart remains with those in jail.

Made in the USA
Lexington, KY
27 September 2018